Language Diversity
and Writing Instruction

Language Diversity and Writing Instruction

Marcia Farr
University of Illinois at Chicago

Harvey Daniels
National College of Education

ERIC Clearinghouse on Urban Education
Institute for Urban and Minority Education
Teachers College/Columbia University
New York, New York 10027

ERIC Clearinghouse on Reading and Communication Skills
National Council of Teachers of English
1111 Kenyon Road, Urbana, Illinois 61801

IUME Consultant Readers: Erwin Flaxman, Charles C. Harrington

NCTE Editorial Board: Candy Carter, Lee Galda-Pellegrini, Donald R. Gallo, Delores Lipscomb, Thomas Newkirk, L. Jane Christensen, *ex officio*, Paul O'Dea, *ex officio*

Staff Editor: Timothy Bryant

Book Design: Tom Kovacs for TGK Design

NCTE Stock Number 26596

Published 1986 by the ERIC Clearinghouse on Urban Education, the Institute for Urban and Minority Education, the ERIC Clearinghouse on Reading and Communication Skills, and the National Council of Teachers of English.

Office of Educational
Research and Improvement
U.S. Department of Education

This publication was prepared with funding from the Office of Educational Research and Improvement, U.S. Department of Education, under contract no. 400-83-0025. Contractors undertaking such projects under government sponsorship are encouraged to express freely their judgment in professional and technical matters. Prior to publication, the manuscript was submitted to the Institute for Urban and Minority Education and the National Council of Teachers of English for critical review and determination of professional competence. This publication has met such standards. Points of view or opinions, however, do not necessarily represent the official view or opinions of either the Institute for Urban and Minority Education, the National Council of Teachers of English, or the Office of Educational Research and Improvement.

Library of Congress Cataloging-in-Publication Data

Farr, Marcia.
   Language diversity and writing instruction.

   Bibliography; p.
   1. English language—Composition and exercises—Study and teaching (Secondary)—United States.
2. English language—Remedial teaching. 3. English language—United States—Standardization. 4. English language—Dialects—United States. I. Daniels, Harvey, 1936-   . II. ERIC Clearinghouse on Urban Education.
III. Title.
PE1405.U6F37 1986   428.2'07'1273   86-24021
ISBN 0-8141-2659-6

Contents

Foreword

The Educational Resources Information Center (ERIC) is a national information system operated by the Office of Educational Research and Improvement (OERI) of the U.S. Department of Education. It provides ready access to descriptions of exemplary programs, research and development efforts, and related information useful in developing effective educational programs. Through its network of specialized centers or clearinghouses, each of which is responsible for a particular educational area, ERIC acquires, evaluates, abstracts, and indexes current significant information and lists this information in its reference publications.

This publication has been jointly developed by the ERIC Clearinghouse on Urban Education and the ERIC Clearinghouse on Reading and Communication Skills. These clearinghouses disseminate educational information related to research, instruction, professional preparation, and policy at all levels and in all institutions.

Through the ERIC Document Reproduction Service the ERIC system has already made available the information collected by the clearinghouses, in the form of research reports, literature reviews, curriculum guides and descriptions, conference papers, project or program reviews, and other print materials related to their scope of interest. However, if the findings of education research, descriptions of practice, and analyses of policy are to be useful to educators, considerable amounts of information and data must be reevaluated, focused, and translated into a different context. OERI has directed the ERIC clearinghouses to work with professional organizations and institutions of higher education to develop information analysis papers on specific areas within their subject scope.

The Institute for Urban and Minority Education, Teachers College/ Columbia University, and the National Council of Teachers of English are pleased to cooperate with OERI in making this book available.

Erwin Flaxman   Charles Suhor
Director, ERIC/UD   Director, ERIC/RCS

Introduction

The goal of this book is to offer both a theoretical framework and some practical suggestions to educators who wish to improve the teaching of writing to high school students who are native speakers of nonstandard English dialects, including adolescents from urban black, bilingual Hispanic, white ethnic, rural, and other linguistically diverse backgrounds. Addressing this urgent educational challenge presents some special problems. In the first place, we do not yet have a substantial body of research bearing directly on the issue of teaching writing to this special group of students. While there are a handful of helpful studies on this topic, the current literature is sketchy and narrow overall. For the time being, our research background must come from two closely related and much better developed fields: research on linguistic variation and the general research on composition instruction. The many studies that have been conducted in these two fields over two decades of energetic research offer significant, if less closely targeted, insights about the teaching of writing to nonstandard-dialect-speaking adolescents. The additional task for educators—and for this book—is to synthesize the findings of linguistic research on nonstandard dialects and instructional research on composition into specific practices for working with real students.

This book is organized around the problem, the relevant research, and the possible solutions. In Chapter 1, we briefly offer some background on the problem of writing in American schools, with special focus on the present writing achievement of nonstandard-dialect-speaking students. In the second chapter, we will review research on language variation, with special emphasis on factors related to the acquisition of literacy. In the final chapter we will present specific suggestions for teaching writing to the students we are concerned with here. These suggestions are the result of applying insights from recent research on both language variation and writing instruction.

1 The Problem of Writing in American Education

We are clearly in a period of intense reexamination of our schools. In recent years, a number of major studies have focused on the state of schooling in our society, particularly at the secondary level. These studies (for example, Boyer 1983, Goodlad 1984, and Sizer 1984) ask both status quo questions (what is the current state of schooling?) and more fundamental questions (what *should* the role of the schools be?). Further evidence of the concern for schools is provided by two large-scale federal efforts to investigate the problem: the congressionally mandated National Assessment of Educational Progress and the National Commission on Excellence. These multiyear projects were charged, in different ways, with assessing how schools and students across the country have been faring in various subject areas.

One of the strongest common themes of all these reports is the recognition of the importance of writing in education, along with concern for the perceived failure of American schools to teach writing effectively. Ernest Boyer, who headed the Carnegie Report on Secondary Education in America, calls literacy "the essential tool":

> The first curriculum priority is language. Our use of complex symbols separates human beings from all other forms of life. Language provides the connecting tissue that binds society together, allowing us to express feelings and ideas, and powerfully influence the attitudes of others. It is the most essential tool for learning. We recommend that high schools help all students develop the capacity to think critically and communicate effectively through the written and spoken word. (p. 85)

Unfortunately, schools don't seem to be providing students with this "essential tool." Boyer cites Applebee's research (1981), which revealed that students do extremely little, and few varied kinds of, writing in school.

Applebee's (1981) investigation of the teaching of writing in secondary schools provided us with a discouraging, though detailed picture:

1. Less than 3 percent of students' time for classwork or homework was devoted to writing a paragraph or more.

3

2. Of the time spent "writing," in English and other classes, students primarily were involved in multiple-choice and short-answer tasks.

3. Very little time was given to prewriting activities or to writing and revising processes, all of which are crucial ingredients in the development of fluency and critical thinking in writing.

4. Finally, even when students were given essays to write, the essays were treated as tests of previous learning rather than as opportunities for them to organize and explore new information.

In a more detailed later study (1984), Applebee offered further evidence of the failure of writing instruction in most American high schools: very little writing of a paragraph or more is assigned in any subject; modes of writing are strictly limited to analysis and summarization; teachers implicitly encourage a first-and-only approach to drafting; students with poor writing skills are no more likely to receive help from their instructors than better writers; and teachers spend more time criticizing students' writing than teaching writing skills.

Both Sizer's and Goodlad's studies reaffirm Boyer's view of the importance of writing in schooling, while adding to Applebee's dismal picture of current instruction. Sizer (1984) emphasizes the importance of writing in learning critical thinking:

> Employing the jargon of logic and practicing what some call "critical thinking" can be intimidating. Effective people, however, use the processes for which these are the labels all the time. . . . One learns these processes, and schools can make this learning efficient. To do so, they must make them explicit and have the students practice with them, as with any skill.
>
> It is in this context that one sees the special importance of writing. One learns complex thinking by practice. There are few certain, easily applied rules for effective thinking; there are, rather, principles with which one wrestles. . . . One thinks, one imagines, one analyzes those ideas, one tests them, and then thinks again. Obviously, unless one has a record of the sequence of one's thoughts, it is difficult to review or analyze them after the fact. A written essay is such a record . . . allowing for dissection. . . . For this reason, exercises in writing should be the center of schooling. (pp. 103–4)

Goodlad (1984) reported that practices in English/language arts and mathematics dominate teaching across the curriculum—that is, they set the norms from which teachers are reluctant to stray. And these practices primarily emphasize basic skills, facts, and mechanics, rather than concepts and "intellectual functions" such as critical thinking. In addition, in the language arts, such skills as

> capitalization, punctuation, paragraphs, syllabification, synonyms, homonyms, antonyms, parts of speech, etc. . . . were repeated in successive grades of the elementary years, were reviewed in the junior high years, and reappeared in the low track classes of the senior high schools. Scattered among these basics were activities suggesting more self-expression and creative thought. . . . (p. 205)

Furthermore, Goodlad distinguishes between what he terms the "explicit" curriculum and the "implicit" curriculum. The primary explicit curriculum for teaching writing is detailed in the quotation above. The implicit curriculum, on the other hand, is taught by *the ways in which the explicit curriculum is presented*—that is, the learning of facts rather than concepts, and displaying knowledge in multiple-choice tests rather than developing new conclusions from learned information. He states,

> Students in the classes we observed made scarcely any decisions about their learning, even though many perceived themselves as doing so. Nearly 100% of the elementary classes were almost entirely teacher dominated with respect to seating, grouping, content, materials, use of space, time utilization, and learning activities. A similar situation prevailed in 90% of the junior high and 80% of the senior high classes. . . . Perhaps students simply expect this and so see themselves as taking part even when their participation in decisons is limited. (p. 229)

Goodlad argues that neither the explicit curriculum nor the implicit curriculum allows students to "become engaged with knowledge so as to employ their full range of intellectual abilities" (p. 231). Unfortunately, his findings add to the evidence that we are not teaching students to think rationally or to evaluate ideas critically. It is no wonder, then, that the writing of most students is considered so inadequate. Good writing, after all, requires thinking and decision making, the active development of thought more than the mechanical display of knowledge. How can students learn to write well if they are primarily being taught to perform repetitive exercises? And, as Goodlad points out, this is even more the pattern in lower-ability tracks than elsewhere. The preponderance of lower-track courses in schools that serve nonstandard-dialect-speaking students makes an examination of the teaching of writing to these pupils particularly urgent.

As we can see, then, the standard procedures for teaching writing in our schools in fact work *against* learning how to write well. And in schools that enroll a large proportion of nonstandard-dialect speakers, the situation is often at its worst. In many inner-city schools, for example, students in lower-ability tracks are repetitively filling out worksheets that ask them to recall information that has been presented to them every year almost since they began school. Rarely are they being challenged actually to write whole pieces of discourse, that is, to evaluate ideas critically, develop disciplined arguments, and express such ideas and arguments in clear and concise written language.

This is the general national situation of writing in American schools, with some indication of the especially grave problem affecting students from nonstandard-dialect-speaking backgrounds. What can be done to improve the situation? Each of the reports cited thus far provides not only information about the status quo but also recommends solutions. In the final chapter of this book we will review these recommendations and other suggestions at length. What can be said here, however, is that much of the improvement must come from increased teacher understanding of the nature of language, of literacy (and particularly of writing), and of learning. This book is intended to facilitate such understanding by synthesizing what we have learned from research on language variation and research on writing instruction.

The answers to the problems described above clearly will not come solely from a new curriculum. Many would argue, in fact, that much would be gained if we eliminated some of the curriculum we already have—for example, the excess worksheets and short-answer tests. Certainly, one key problem is that most teachers teaching in schools today have never been taught to teach writing. Donald Graves's report to the Ford Foundation (1978), based on a survey of schools of education, indicated that only rarely is a course on the teaching of writing included in preservice programs for teachers. Since that time, there has been some movement to improve teacher preparation, but such courses are still the exception rather than the rule. In any case, such changes can only affect the education of new teachers. Those already teaching can be reached primarily through inservice courses and special institutes. Here, too, we have seen some improvement, with the 130 sites of the National Writing Project often leading the way. There is, nevertheless, a long way to go to improve the preparation of writing teachers, as studies such as Applebee's, Goodlad's and Sizer's amply document.

We hope that this book will be a contribution to such teacher growth and renewal. We can envision it being used by individual teachers who wish to gain a better understanding of this complex instructional issue, or as a text in an inservice program on the teaching of writing to nonstandard-dialect-speaking students. While we realize that information does not by itself enable a teacher to develop new classroom practices, we believe that a background in research and theory is one vital ingredient in any teacher's reconsideration of his or her work.

2 Language Variation and Literacy

Understanding the nature of language and the human capacity for language learning and use is a crucial part of the knowledge teachers need. Since learning in schools occurs primarily through language, this kind of knowledge is important in all subject areas, but it is vital in literacy instruction. Though definitions vary, literacy obviously involves the use of written language. Using written language to write and to read is, at a minimum, using one's linguistic competence. In other words, learning and using written language, because of the common language base, has much in common with learning and using oral language. Thus we can improve literacy instruction by increasing our understanding of language and of the complex human capacities for learning and using it.

In this chapter we will review what is known about the linguistic capacities of all human beings; we do this in detail because it is a crucial first step toward analyzing and improving writing instruction. An in-depth understanding of these matters will enable teachers of writing to implement the pedagogical suggestions presented in our final chapter as a natural course of events. That is, the specific suggestions for teachers in the last chapter flow naturally from a detailed understanding of the nature of linguistic competence and of patterned variation in the language of students.

The Linguistic Capacities of All Speakers

There are two primary perspectives from which linguists have studied language: one that focuses on *similarities* across all languages, and one that focuses on *differences* in the languages used by different groups of people. The former perspective seeks to define universals in language and in human language capacities. In this view, language is an aspect of being human, a genetic endowment. Through studies of languages across the world, linguists have been able to identify a number of "language universals," characteristics which are shared by all the languages studied so far. Thus, according to Greenberg (1963),

9

> Underlying the endless and fascinating idiosyncrasies of the
> world's languages there are uniformities of universal scope. Amid
> infinite diversity, all languages are, as it were, cut from the same
> pattern. . . . Language universals are by their very nature sum-
> mary statements about characteristics or tendencies shared by all
> human speakers. (p. xv)

In a review of linguistic theory for the concerns of bilingual education, Ferguson (1977) describes research that has identified some language universals:

> Linguists have found that the internal structure of languages
> (phonology, syntax, etc.) reflects a universal framework, has uni-
> versal properties and exhibits universal tendencies of change,
> although the differences between languages may be very great
> within these universal limits. Thus, all languages have some way
> to express transitive propositions of the sort "John (Subject)–hit
> (Verb)–the ball (Object)," but in some languages (e.g., Japanese
> and Turkish) the normal order is SOV, in others (e.g., Biblical
> Hebrew and Classical Arabic) it is VSO, and in English and most
> European languages it is SVO. All languages have at least some
> "relator" words (e.g., *under, through, with*) used with nouns, and
> in SOV languages these normally come after the noun ("table
> under"), while in VSO and SVO languages they normally come
> before the noun ("under table"). . . . In all languages, expressions
> of time are based on expressions of spatial relations (*in* a box, *in*
> five minutes). . . . (p. 46)

Such findings support the theory that all human beings have a
genetic capacity to learn and use a language. Thus, as Chomsky (1965)
argued, human beings seem to be born with a "language-acquisition
device," which enables them to learn a complex system of knowledge
(a particular language) in a relatively short time. He claimed that the
"underlying regularities" which are universal must be part of a
child's innate capacities; otherwise, the feat of language acquisition
which all children achieve when they learn the particular language
of their community simply by being exposed to it for a few years
would not be possible.

Chomsky used the term *linguistic competence* to refer to the
abstract system of knowledge which all children acquire and which
all speakers of a language must have in order to use their language.
He pointed out, furthermore, that this is not conscious knowledge;
instead, it is an underlying system of rules which is *unconsciously*
known by the speaker. It is this underlying system which is utilized
by the speaker in linguistic performance (speaking). In Chomsky's
(1965) words,

Obviously, every speaker of a language has mastered and internalized a generative grammar that expresses his knowledge of his language. This is not to say that he is aware of the rules of the grammar or even that he can become aware of them, or that his statements about his intuitive knowledge of the language are necessarily accurate. . . . [We are] dealing, for the most part, with mental processes that are far beyond the level of actual or even potential consciousness; furthermore, it is quite apparent that a speaker's reports and viewpoints about his behavior and his competence may be in error. Thus a generative grammar attempts to specify what the speaker actually knows, not what he may report about his knowledge. (p. 8)

So linguistic competence is what a speaker *actually knows,* and the evidence of this knowledge is found in the everyday fact of one's linguistic performance, that is, in speaking the language of one's community. Furthermore, *every speaker of every language* has such linguistic competence, including both the genetic endowment of linguistic capacity and the internalized system of knowledge which enables him or her to communicate verbally. Hartwell (1985) provides a simple example of this implicit competence: he asks native speakers of English to explain the rule for ordering (before a noun) adjectives of nationality, age, and number. Native speakers, who use such a rule regularly, are unable to explain it immediately upon demand. Then he presents them with the following five words and asks them to put the words in order:

French   the   young   girls   four

Native speakers of English, regardless of dialect (a point we will return to shortly), are able to perform this exercise quickly, naturally, and unanimously. This is evidence that all these speakers share unconscious knowledge of a "rule" which describes the appropriate order of such adjectives in English. They may not "know" that they know this rule, but they clearly do, for they are able to put such knowledge to use in speaking and understanding English. The above exercise is a simplified example of a "linguistic rule"; most such rules are much more complex and not so easily brought to conscious awareness. Nevertheless, this example serves well as a concrete illustration of how speakers of a language know much more than they think they know.

An example from Labov (1970) provides an even clearer understanding of what the linguistic rules of a speaker's linguistic competence actually are like. Labov emphasizes that using language is far from a simple process; it is, in fact, "a complex process of translating meanings or intentions into sound" (p. 7). To exemplify this complex process, Labov details the linguistic rules English speakers must know in order to produce and understand a particular senténce:

> Let us consider such a sentence as *John wants to know how you like him.* As it is spoken, it consists of a chain of eight words in succession. But it conveys a complex message containing at least three distinct propositions. The dominant sentence is that *John wants something.* What is that something? It is *to know something else.* There is no immediate subject of *know*—it has been deleted by a regular rule—but it is plainly John who is *to know something else.* And that something else is *the extent to which,* or *how you like him.* We can suggest the complexity of this sentence by a diagram such as the following:

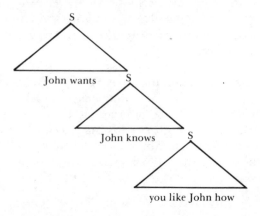

> It might be possible for a language to glue these three proposi- tions together by simple adjunction into something like *John wants John knows you like John how.* But we never hear any- thing like this; every schoolchild is in control of a complex series of deletions, substitutions, and foregroundings which produce *John wants to know how you like him.* To produce this sentence he must at least
>
> 1. Attach the second sentence to the first as an infinitive with *for . . . to* as complementizer
>   John wants for (John) to know . . .
> 2. Drop the second *John* as identical with the first
>   John wants for . . . to know . . .
> 3. Drop the first half of the complementizer *for*
>   John wants to know . . .
> 4. Bring the question word *how* in the third sentence to the front
>   John wants to know how you like John . . .
> 5. Convert this *John* into the appropriate pronoun *him.*
>   (pp. 7–8)

This example underscores the complexity of linguistic competence, that is, how elaborate the organization of linguistic rules is in any language. Human languages are extremely intricate systems, as numerous studies of them have attested. No language yet has been completely analyzed and described; the complexity in both structure and use so far has exceeded the understanding of linguistic scholars. And yet, succeeding generations of children learn these elaborate, interlocking systems of rules fairly easily and quickly. Furthermore, children learn language without being explicitly taught the "rules"; they learn it through exposure and use.

So far we have explored some of the universal aspects of linguistic competence. Such universals tell us about similarities across all varieties of human language and verify the linguistic capacities of all normal human beings. This means that teachers can assume such capacities, and a highly developed linguistic system as well, for all their students. Excluding a very small percentage of people who have genuine language disabilities (and such students generally are not in regular classrooms), this is true regardless of other varying individual abilities, such as IQ.

Language Differences across Dialects

American schools enroll students from a wide range of backgrounds, and this diversity is reflected in linguistic and other cultural norms. So while all students have a highly developed linguistic competence, or set of underlying rules, which enables them to use their language, they do not share exactly the *same* set of rules. A language (English, for example) is not in reality one nonvarying system which all speakers share and all children for whom it is a native language learn. Although the vast majority of the rules are shared by all speakers of English, there are also systematic differences in rules for various dialects of English. Within dialects, each speaker has an orderly set of rules which accounts for the language he or she produces. However, that particular set of rules is not shared by all speakers of English, or even all speakers of the same dialect.

Let us consider what a dialect actually is and how the various dialects of a language relate to each other. The term *dialect* has been used primarily to refer to a regional variety of a language which differs from other varieties of that language primarily in matters of vocabulary and pronunciation. By interviewing people in various regions and analyzing their language, dialectologists are able to distinguish one regional dialect from another. When some linguists began to study language differences which characterized various social, rather than regional, groups of people, *dialect* was extended to refer to the variety of a language used by a particular group of speakers, whether that group was identified regionally (e.g., "southern English speakers") or socially (Vernacular Black English speakers).

It is important to realize that the term *dialect* is actually an abstract concept—it is not a nonvarying language system used by a finite group of speakers. People shift in and out of formal and informal styles of speaking depending upon whom they are talking to, the context within which they are speaking, what they are talking about, and so on. Thus, though each speaker of a language (or a dialect) does have a self-contained linguistic system which he or she uses to communicate verbally, a particular dialect (or a language, for that matter) is not in reality a system which exists identically in all speakers' minds. Variation in the rules of a language, or, more often, slightly different versions of the same rules, distinguish speakers according to region, social status, sex, ethnicity, age, and other factors. As sets of these variations are studied and described by linguists, they are identified as features which are characteristic of the language use of a particular group of people and called a "dialect."

This is not to say that there is not a great deal of convergence in linguistic features used by a particular group of people. These characteristic features are shared to a great extent, and so can be said to comprise the dialect in question. In recent years, however, the term *dialect* often has been taken too literally, with confusion the result. To dispel such confusion, we can clarify terms such as *dialect* by specifying what they mean with concrete examples from linguistic studies. In turn, this will enable us to be more realistic about the nature of language variation in planning educational strategies for teachers.

What does it mean to be able to "speak a dialect"? It certainly means that, in general terms, one has in one's linguistic repertoire those features which are characteristic of the dialect. Some speakers may use most of the features of a dialect but at a lower frequency of occurrence than do others, who may be what Baugh (1983) has termed true "vernacular speakers"—those who live, work, and play among speakers of the same vernacular. Thus, even within a much-studied and highly recognizable dialect such as Vernacular Black English (also called Black English Vernacular, as below), there is considerable variation in the use of dialect features by different speakers.

Labov and Harris (1983) define Black English as follows:

> We use the term *Black English* to describe . . . the full range of language used by Black people in the United States. The term *Black English Vernacular* (BEV) is a linguistic term, not a social term. It refers to the highly consistent grammar, pronunciation and lexicon that is the first dialect learned by most black people throughout the United States, and used in much the same way by adults in their most intimate home settings with family and friends. (p. 6)

They mean by this that BEV, as an example of one among many dialects in the United States, is a linguistic description of particular features of language which are characteristically used by working-class black Americans. They do not mean that the dialect described in linguistic studies as BEV is used categorically by a finite group of speakers—e.g., all black Americans, or even all working-class black Americans. Thus the term has a *linguistic* referent, not a social one. Many such linguistic descriptions, representing many dialects, together make up what has been called the *sociolinguistic structure of English*. This structure allows for variation not only across dialects but also within dialects.

Language Variation within Dialects

Most people are sensitive to differences in language patterns across dialects; that is, they can recognize certain language patterns as characterizing "Black English," "southern English," or other dialects of English. In addition to this kind of regional and social variation, there is substantial variation *within* dialects. Some of this variation is patterned according to characteristics of the particular speaker (e.g., gender, age, social class), and some of it is patterned according to characteristics of the context in which the language is being used.

A good example of the former (variation according to speaker characteristics) is the varying frequency with which multiple negatives have been found to be used by males and females from different social classes. The following figure is taken from Wolfram and Fasold's (1974) study of black speech in Detroit. Though the data are specific to this study, this kind of patterning has been replicated numerous times elsewhere. In this figure, we can see that multiple negatives (e.g., *He didn't do nothin' about it*) are used with the highest frequency by males from the lower working class. In contrast,

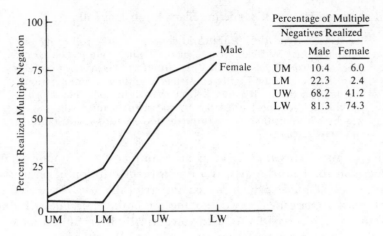

Figure 1. Percentage of realized multiple negation: by social class and sex (Wolfram and Fasold 1974, p. 93).

multiple negatives are used with the lowest frequency by females from the upper middle class. The figures for frequency of occurrence are obtained by calculating the number of times (in speech sampled for the study) speakers actually used multiple negatives out of the total number of times they could have done so (i.e., used structures of negation which allowed for multiple realization). This figure clearly illustrates that how often a speaker actually uses a "dialect feature" like multiple negation depends in part upon whether the speaker is male or female and upon which social class the speaker belongs to.

Variation within a dialect according to context is harder to measure, since contexts can be defined according to a wide variety of aspects, including time, place, participants (including status and role relationships), and topic, among other things. One aspect of context that has been measured, however, is its relative formality, and, correspondingly, the relative formality of the language being used. The following figure illustrates data taken from Labov's (1964) study of the use of the postvocalic *r* (e.g., in the word *four*) in New York City speech. He analyzed language samples ranging from casual speech to the reading of words in pairs, and classified speakers into socioeconomic classes according to such factors as occupation and income.

This figure is interesting for a number of reasons. First, it clearly illustrates that how frequently New York City speakers use *r* depends both upon their social class and upon the relative formality of the language style they are using. The *r* is included most frequently in the most formal styles and least frequently in the most informal

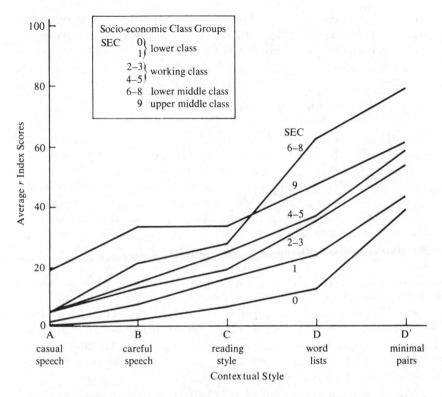

Figure 2. Class stratification diagram for *r* (Labov 1964, p. 171). Reproduced by permission of the American Anthropological Association from *American Anthropologist* 66:6, Part 2, 1964. Not for further reproduction.

styles. A second interesting aspect of this figure is the pattern of "hypercorrection" by the lower-middle-class speakers. This pattern has been interpreted to reflect the desire by lower-middle-class speakers to be considered upper middle class; through their speech, they unconsciously reflect this desire by "outdoing" even the upper-middle-class speakers in using a feature characteristically associated with both formality and higher class status.

Figures 1 and 2 represent typical results from numerous studies of language variation during the past two decades. This body of research has documented variation within many dialects, including Black English, Puerto Rican English, varieties of Native American English, Appalachian English, Chicano English, and both southern and northern varieties of nonstandard white dialects. There are two major findings from all this work that are important for teachers of writing:

first, such variation is not random, but is patterned according to a number of factors; second, a "dialect" is not a monolithic entity, and a "dialect speaker" does not categorically use all dialect features all the time.

Inherent Variability and Variable Rules

Even those who are considered "true vernacular speakers" of a dialect do not use all the features characteristic of that dialect 100 percent of the time, even within the most conducive contexts. In addition to variation which occurs because of the context in which the language is being used, there is linguistically determined variation in the use of particular features by all speakers. This kind of variation was termed *inherent variability* by Labov (1969), and it is an important concept for those involved in language and literacy instruction. This term essentially refers to the fact that the linguistic context of a particular feature (e.g., whether a vowel or a consonant follows a potential *-ed* suffix) determines to a certain extent whether or not that feature will be realized in a particular utterance in a person's speech. This means that a certain amount of variability is *inherent* in linguistic competence, and not just the result of the situation in which language is being used. This kind of variability is accounted for in linguistic theory by what Labov termed *variable rules.*

A variable rule is a kind of linguistic rule which only operates under certain conditions. Those linguistic rules which do not operate variably (such as those involved in ordering adjectives or producing *John wants to know how you like him*) are called *obligatory rules;* that is, they always operate in distinguishing (for example) an English sentence from a non-English sentence. If they operated variably, the utterances would not be considered English by any native speakers, regardless of dialect. Variable rules, on the other hand, describe the linguistic patterning which allows the feature to be realized variably rather than categorically. Before Labov identified such patterning in language use, all variation was ascribed to "optional rules" that allowed for what was called "free variation." Although such free variation operated presumably according to speaker choice, no linguists up to that time actually had investigated it to search for patterning, that is, to see if it were rule-governed. The identification of variable rules was a major advance in linguistic theory and provides an excellent example of the complexity of linguistic competence. To make this important concept concrete, we have provided a simplified example of a variable rule below (this is taken from a more detailed explanation in Wolfram and Fasold 1974, Chapter 5).

Let us consider the variable rule for contraction in English as defined by Labov (1969, p. 748). Contraction is actually removal of the vowel in *am, is, are*—leaving *'m, 's, 're* (e.g., *I'm here, He's writing, You're ugly*). There are certain conditions that *must* be met in order for this rule to operate (e.g., the vowel to be removed must be unaccented). Certain other conditions can be present or not, but their presence *favors* the operation of the rule (e.g., if a verb follows the word that may be contracted, as in *He is going* rather than *He is good*). In fact, for this particular variable rule, there are three constraints that affect its output:

1. The rule is favored if a verb follows (e.g., *John is going* is more likely to undergo contraction than *John is good* or *John is a man*).

2. The rule is favored if the preceding word ends in a vowel (e.g., *Joe is going* is favored over *John is going*).

3. The rule is favored if the following constituent, if not a verb, is a noun phrase (e.g., *John is a man* is favored over *John is good* or *John is in Chicago*).

Constraints such as these for variable rules are identified by careful analysis of language samples taken from a group of speakers. By counting the number of times contraction occurs in various combinations of the above three linguistic contexts, the researcher can rank the constraints which favor contraction in a hierarchy, from the highest frequency of occurrence to the lowest (in this case, from 86 percent to 25 percent). All of these factors—the necessary conditions as well as the favoring constraints—are ultimately incorporated into a formal variable rule (of the transformational-generative type formulated by Chomsky) for linguistic theory. Linguists differ in their exact formulations of variable rules (e.g., some incorporate social constraints such as ethnicity into the formal linguistic rule), but they do not disagree about the empirical validity of the rules.

For those involved in literacy instruction, knowing the actual details of one variable rule or another is not as important as understanding the concept of inherent variability, and especially how this concept illustrates the complexity of linguistic competence for all speakers. This is particularly important for those working in urban schools, where a variety of nonstandard-dialect speakers are commonly misperceived as being linguistically undeveloped or inadequate.

Even those who do not categorize nonstandard-dialect speakers as linguistically undeveloped or deficient often misinterpret the variation they hear in a student's language use. Several researchers (Perl 1980, Bartholomae 1984, Hartwell 1985) have shown that many students, when reading aloud what they have written, will often "correct" the nonstandard features in their writing to standard English pronunciations, frequently without realizing that what they have read aloud differs from what they had written. These researchers interpret this behavior as evidence that students actually "know" standard English features and can correct most of their nonstandard patterns to standard ones (and therefore that the teaching of standard English grammar is unnecessary).

When such student behavior is interpreted in the light of sociolinguistic studies of language variation, however, alternative explanations emerge. Reading aloud is a more formal style of using language than is casual speaking, as is shown in Figure 2 above. Consequently, it is predictable that reading aloud would evidence a higher frequency of standard English features than would casual speaking, and, possibly, first-draft writing. Moreover, unless the specific linguistic contexts (e.g., following consonants or vowels) for each occurrence are examined, the role of the inherent variability of each feature in such student behavior is unclear. In sum, the reasons for using either the standard or the nonstandard variant of a particular feature are not as simple as they might appear. Students' "corrections" of nonstandard forms may only be indications of deeply conditioned language variation, of the sort amply documented in sociolinguistic studies of various dialects.

This is not to say, of course, that the formal teaching of standard English grammar is therefore the best approach to teaching this aspect of writing in urban schools. It is clear, however, from studies by Labov and others, that such variation in the use of nonstandard features is an inherent part of such speakers' linguistic competence and is not evidence that they already "know" standard English rules. Many students do not know how to correct nonstandard features in their writing and, even when highly motivated to learn to write standard English, are quite puzzled about which features in their writing to change. For these students, conscious awareness of standard and nonstandard rules may be necessary for them to learn to write using standard English. The question remaining is *how* the rules should be approached in the classroom, not whether or not they should be.

Researchers such as Perl, Bartholomae, and Hartwell may be accurate in their indictment of decades of traditional approaches to the teaching of standard grammar. These approaches clearly have not been effective, particularly in urban schools with nonstandard-dialect speakers. Yet there is no convincing evidence that writing teachers should abandon the effort to help nonstandard-dialect-speaking students come to conscious awareness and control of the features of standard English grammar. On the contrary, as we outline in the next chapter, there is much that teachers can and should do to help their students make use of these linguistic features.

Nonstandard Dialects and Standard English

All languages, even those with a small number of speakers, have dialects (Ferguson 1977) that serve to identify speakers in either geographical or social space. In linguistic terms, the degree to which dialects differ from one another (whether differences are slight or more extensive) varies from language to language. It is clear, however, that there are more rules that dialects have in common than there are rules that distinguish dialects. This is represented in Figure 3, which illustrates the relation among dialects of American English.

Quite apart from the linguistic differences among dialects is the social value placed on different dialects. The clearest example of this in our own society is the higher value placed on the dialect we call "standard English" than on various nonstandard American English dialects (e.g., Vernacular Black English, Appalachian English, Puerto Rican English, etc.).

The question of whether or not standard English is actually a dialect has been raised by a number of scholars. That is, does the term *standard English* identify a group of speakers with particular linguistic features? Or, more plausibly, does *standard English* simply refer,

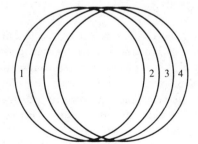

1. Standard English
2. Northern white nonstandard English
3. Southern white nonstandard English
4. Vernacular Black English

Figure 3. Relationship among dialects of American English (Wolfram and Fasold 1974, p. 34).

for most people, to language use that avoids those stigmatized features that are identified with nonstandard dialects? Although a number of writers have referred rather facilely to standard English as a "dialect" over the years, increasing evidence from linguistic studies has illuminated the range of variation (much of which might not be considered standard by teachers of writing) in the speech of educated upper-middle-class people in our society. Also, as Taylor (1983) has pointed out, there is a linguistically describable Standard Black English, as well as a Vernacular Black English (the former utilizing standard grammar with elements of black verbal style). There are, then, different kinds of "standard English" in our society which are appropriate in particular situations of language use.

The notion that there is a single standard English is considerably weakened by the fact that there are so many different versions of such a standard. Although every dialect contains abundant variation, there is a point at which variation around an ideal, or a norm, defies the existence of the norm. This seems to be the case for varieties of oral "standard" English. But what about a written standard? Is there a written standard English?

Hirsch (1977), quoting Haugen (1966), refers to standard English as a *grapholect*—apparently a variety of a language which is *not* a dialect, but is the "national written language" of a country. His argument, while appealing in some respects, relies on two assumptions that are problematic: first, that a dialect is an oral form of language:

> A national language such as Italian or English is not a dialect at all in the sense that the purely oral language of a speech community is a dialect. It is a different *kind* of language system. . . .
> (p. 43)

The problem here is that although traditional studies of dialects have been of oral language, written language is not precluded by definition. For example, there are numerous uses of "dialects" in both fiction (Traugott 1981) and poetry.

Secondly, in relying on work by the Russian linguist M. M. Guxman, Hirsch seems to be assuming that dialects are by definition not only oral but *regional* varieties of a language. From studying the development of a number of national written languages, Guxman concluded that "the written norm is never in fact the simple codification of a system of dialect characteristics of any one region" (Hirsch 1977, p. 43). This may be the case in terms of the origins of many national written languages, but it doesn't prove that written standards aren't simply another variety of a language, or a set of ways for using a particular language. Nevertheless, Hirsch concludes, on these bases, that a written standard is not a class-based dialect, or as Sledd (1972) has indicated, "a dialect with an army and a navy." Instead, Hirsch sees the standard English grapholect as "a transdialectal construct" which rightly contains norms of correctness for the entire language. In this way Hirsch justifies the *linguistic* superiority of standard written English. Although claiming that a grapholect is not a dialect partly because it is not oral, he associates the grapholect with, strangely enough, a "phonology," and thus claims the grapholect as the "transcendent norm of speech," or, in other words, the correct way to speak.

Unfortunately, such reasoning is based on unclear notions of such concepts as "dialect" and "linguistic system," as well as on a lack of specificity about how language actually is used. We have defined the term *dialect* above according to the results of empirical studies of language use: it is a linguistic description of a variety of a language that characterizes a group of speakers in either geographic or social space. There is no reason to assume that a written standard, or grapholect, couldn't be described linguistically. However, this remains an empirical question, not a philosophical one. Written standards certainly have "vocabulary layers" and "syntactic peculiarities" (as Hirsch quotes Guxman as determining) which don't typically exist in most speakers' oral language use. But since dialects need not be, by definition, either purely oral or solely regional, a grapholect could be considered a dialect, and not a different *kind* of linguistic system. In fact, by definition, a literate person's linguistic competence—or language system—must include knowledge of such matters as "literate" vocabulary and syntax.

It seems safe to conclude, then, that while there appears to be no codified oral standard English appropriate for use in all contexts, there may be a written standard, termed by some a grapholect, which, even with its variations, is largely appropriate in various contexts across space and time. The linguistic description of this "dialect," or grapholect, is not yet complete, although some researchers have made a start (e.g., Chafe 1982). As in any attempt to describe dialects, it will be important to note the kind and amount of variation, even among the literati (e.g., stylistic preferences), which is appropriate and acceptable. Thus, even a written standard, while it might be regarded as a dialect, is not a monolithic code, but a code with variations.

When we teach "standard English," then, we are teaching, in part, avoidance of stigmatized features associated with nonstandard dialects.

We are also teaching new ways of using language that are characteristic of the grapholect or dialect of those who immerse themselves
in certain kinds of written language—what some would term the
"academic subculture" of our society. It is important to remember in
both cases that "nonstandard" ways of using language are stigmatized
because they are associated with dialects of lesser political, economic,
or social value, not because they are any less adequate linguistically.
Also, it should be clear from the preceding discussion of linguistic
competence that such ways of using language are deeply ingrained
aspects of a speaker's internal language system. As such, they are not
easily changed through direct teaching—a point that has been made
clear through decades of instruction in English and language arts
classes. The lack of such change is puzzling to many teachers, especially in the case of students who clearly see a need for and are working hard to learn the ways of "standard English."

Cultural Differences

Most students who begin school as nonstandard-dialect speakers leave
school without acquiring standard written English, despite the fact
that they have spent up to twelve years in a context in which it is
taught. A number of explanations have been offered for this peculiar
phenomenon, some of them social and cultural, and others linguistic.
Many of these explanations share the assumption of a conflict between
communicative systems, that is, between the ways the students use
language at home and in their communities and the ways they are
expected to use language in school.

Before discussing the potential conflicts between communicative
systems, however, we'd like to note some other possible explanations
which may underlie these conflicts. Ogbu (1974, 1980) has linked the
problems which minority children face inside classrooms to broader
problems of caste status and racism in the larger society of which
schools are a part. Thus he calls for research which takes into account
the world outside of classrooms, rather than focusing on micro-
interactions within classrooms. Gilmore and Smith (1982), acknowledging Ogbu's concern, have questioned why children, faced with
unfamiliar ways of communicating, don't eventually adapt to the new
situation and learn the new ways of using oral and written language.
The fact that children don't adapt leads these researchers to conclude
that there may be a systemic reason for it within the culture of
the school. From this perspective, some students may choose to fail

because the personal costs of learning to become members of the school culture are seen as too high.

In addition to locating the problem within cultural systems, either in the larger society or within the subculture of the classroom, negative teacher attitudes toward nonstandard dialects (and by extension toward those who use them) have been identified by many as a large part of the problem. Farr Whiteman (1980) and Chambers (1983) have explored the controversial "Ann Arbor Case." In this federal court case, a group of parents of Vernacular Black English-speaking elementary school students brought suit against the Ann Arbor, Michigan, public schools. The parents claimed that the schools were denying their children's civil rights by failing to teach them to read and write standard English. After extensive testimony by linguists and others on the extant research, Judge Harold Joiner ruled in the parents' favor in 1979. The expert testimony pointed both to linguistic differences between Vernacular Black English and standard English and to negative attitudes toward nonstandard dialects as key causes of the school's failure. The remedy required by the court was inservice education designed to inform teachers about the linguistic adequacy of nonstandard dialects and to turn teachers' negative attitudes into more positive ones.

Thus there are a number of related social explanations for the fact that so many students from nonmainstream subcultures fail to become literate in our schools. These explanations are not as concrete nor as obvious as differences among communicative systems between various nonmainstream groups and the mainstream middle class. Differences in communicative systems lead to both cultural conflict and linguistic conflict in the classroom. In the rest of this and the following section we will explore each of these areas in detail.

Among the "cultural conflict" explanations offered is one suggested by Labov (1972a): peer-group status among adolescents is associated with vernacular dialects, at least in the inner city. In a study of the relation of reading failure to peer-group status among adolescents in Harlem, Labov found that peer-group leaders who demonstrated (outside of school) all the scholastic and verbal ability needed to succeed in school still did not do so. He concluded that these teenagers had "turned their backs on school culture" because it conflicted with the street culture in which they were firmly grounded. Although Labov (1972a, 1983) also argues that there are structural (linguistic) differences between standard English and Vernacular Black English which do cause some problems in learning written standard English, he maintains that the primary conflict is a cultural one.

Because literacy is an essential goal of schooling, students who reject schooling in essence reject literacy—or, at least, society's perceived primary opportunity for them to become literate. Yet not all inner-city students reject the school culture. Some try hard to do well in school, perhaps to live up to well-documented parental expectations (Heath 1983, among others) that doing well in school will lead to "success." Even these students, however, if they come from a non-mainstream culture, largely fail to become literate. Thus we are faced with an apparent enigma: given the complex linguistic capacities of all human beings, why should these students fail in this process, when they clearly have succeeded in learning to speak the language of their community? As we have seen above, linguistic capacity in itself is tremendously complex. The question we must ask, then, is this: why is becoming literate often so difficult, whereas learning to speak one's native language is not?

In order to begin answering this question, we must explore what literacy is. A number of researchers began to investigate the nature of literacy by following the suggestion of Goody and Watt (1963) that the development of literacy has both cultural and cognitive consequences. They argued, on the basis of the historical development of Western civilization, that literacy changes both societies and individuals—that is, becoming literate affects how people use language and how they think. Initially, researchers exploring literacy and its "opposite," orality, defined typical characteristics of the two modes of language in terms of a dichotomy. For example, Olson (1977) claimed that for written language meaning resides primarily in the text itself, whereas for oral language much meaning is communicated in the context in which the language is used. In this sense, then, written language is more autonomous, or decontextualized, than spoken language.

Olson's work, and other work along these lines, seems to be based on a characterization of oral language as casual conversation and of written language as the (Western) school essay, not on the full range of *kinds* of oral and written language that more recent research has documented. For example, researchers such as Scollon and Scollon (1981), Tannen (1982b), Heath (1983), and Street (1984) have shown that all language use, whether oral or written, is embedded in a social context which affects both its form and its function. Furthermore, these researchers and others have illustrated how language use in a literate society draws on aspects of orality and literacy in subtle and overlapping ways. In other words, speaking and writing are alternate ways of using one's language capacities, and very often both modes are used within a single speech or literacy "event."

Heath (1983) describes in detail the ways in which children from two neighboring communities in the Piedmont area of North Carolina are socialized into the ways of using oral and written language which are characteristic of each group. In doing so, she illustrates why it is necessary to understand the beliefs and conceptual principles by which people live in order fully to understand their language practices. That is, the ways people use oral and written language are inextricably bound up with other patterns characteristic of their culture. For example, Heath contrasts the language socialization process in the two nonmainstream communities, one she calls Trackton (a black working-class rural southern community) and one she calls Roadville (a white working-class rural southern community).

According to Heath, Trackton children learn how to talk "on their own," as it were. For the first year of a Trackton baby's life, he or she is carried around or held constantly on laps. Babies are not spoken to (unlike in other communities, where "baby talk" is used while talking to a baby, even when the baby is clearly not old enough to respond). The language and social life of the community are there to be observed by the baby, however, since babies are rarely alone during the first year of their lives; instead, they are almost continuously a part of the ongoing stream of interaction among the members of their families and community.

In this early period, as well as later on, Trackton children learn to place high reliance on context, and particularly on nonverbal cues, in negotiating language interactions with other members of their community. Thus they learn to be flexible and adaptable in their use of language, depending upon constantly changing situations and cues. They learn to switch roles with other members of the community, imitating the roles of others in verbal play. In this community, as in some other black communities (Kochman 1972a, 1981), creative verbal play, with frequent metaphors and similes, is highly valued. There is also a sustained focus, both in language use and in other aspects of the culture, on interpersonal relationships. Details in the context are assumed to be of prime importance, and children frequently ask questions that place items in a more fully developed context:

> Establishing the context of any newly introduced item—where it came from, whose it is, and how it is used—is often the purpose of Trackton children's questions. When introduced to a new item which is called by a name they use for reference to a different

object, they try to test the extent of similarities between the old and the new. For example, in Trackton Text IV, Benjy, hearing "block" used to refer to something unfamiliar to him, tested his own definition of block in an operational way. He did not know a city block, but he did know the term *block* as referring to scraps of lumber. When I used the term *block* to mean city block, he issued a series of questions and challenges to establish how similar the new referent was to that one which he knew. (p. 107)

Heath continues her description of this cultural pattern in Trackton:

> Trackton children, however, never volunteer to list the attributes which are similar in two objects and add up to make one thing like another. They seem, instead, to have a gestalt, a highly contextualized view, of objects which they compare without sorting out the particular single features of the object itself. They seem to become sensitive to the shape of arrays of stimuli in a scene, but not to how individual discrete elements in the scene contribute to making two wholes alike. If asked why or how one thing is like another, they do not answer; similarly, they do not respond appropriately to tasks in which they are asked to distinguish one thing as different from another. (pp. 107–8)

This pattern of seeing an object holistically in context, rather than as an accumulation of attributes, does not serve the Trackton children well in the early years of school, where the naming of attributes of objects (e.g., colors and shapes) is a common activity. Heath's thorough ethnographic study of this community also documented the fact that Trackton children have no experience with answering questions about the attributes of objects, a fact which is commented on by a Trackton grandmother: "We don't talk to our chil'ren like you folks do. We don't ask 'em 'bout colors, names, 'n things" (p. 109). Thus Trackton adults acknowledge that they do not bring up their children as mainstream parents do, talking about objects in the world; instead, they let children learn how to talk and how to become participating members of their community by their own means—that is, the children are expected to learn by observing and then participating, and they do.

Although Trackton children have other ways of using language which should serve them well in school (e.g., creativity in the use of rhymes and metaphors), their early experiences in school, where written language is often taught as a series of subskills, confuse and discourage them, so that they never progress to the point in school where these more innovative uses of language are more evident in the school curriculum. Moreover, some students seem to get stuck in the remedial track, continuously repeating exercises on, but never "mastering," what are presumed to be the subskills necessary to learn written language.

In the other nonmainstream community which Heath describes, the one she calls Roadville, the language socialization process is quite different. The white working-class adults believe that they "teach" their children how to talk and how to learn before they begin formal schooling. Babies are regularly talked to, both by parents and by older siblings, even before they are able to respond. Baby talk is used often in these interactions, even when no one else is around to receive a secondary message from utterances seemingly addressed to the baby. In contrast to the pattern in Trackton, babies in Roadville are usually either alone with their mothers, experiencing much baby talk inter-action, or they are left to themselves, to explore, move about, or babble on their own. A baby's sounds are listened to expectantly for signs of the baby learning the names of people and things in his or her world; sometimes the baby's "word" for something is taken up and used by the whole family.

In verbal interactions with babies, Roadville mothers treat their babies as though they are participating in the interactions, both as "information-givers" and as "information-receivers." Much emphasis is put upon babies learning to name objects around them and, even-tually, upon learning how to name the attributes (e.g., colors and shapes) of various objects. Heath describes this pattern:

> When the baby begins to respond verbally, to make sounds which adults can link to items in the environment, questions and statements are addressed to the baby, repeating or incorporating his "word." This practice is carried out with not only first chil-dren, but also subsequent children, and when adults are not around to do it, older children take up the game of repeating children's sounds as words and pointing out new items in the environment and asking babies to "say ——." When Sally, Aunt Sue's youngest child, began saying "ju, ju, ju" from her infant seat and high chair, Lisa, her older sister, said "Juice, juice, Mamma, she wants some of my juice, can I give it to her?" Lisa also named other items for Sally: "Milk, say milk," and when Sally discovered a sesame seed on the tray of her high chair and tried to pick it up, Lisa said "Seed, see:d, that's a seed, can you say see::d?" There is verbal reinforcement and smiles and cuddling when the baby repeats. (p. 122)

Thus in Roadville, in direct contrast with Trackton, babies begin almost immediately to "participate" in dialogues with others, rather than being left to "figure things out" on their own. The children of both communities, of course, learn how to talk at a normal rate of development, but the context in which they learn to do so differs markedly from one community to the other. The Trackton grandmother who said, "We don't talk to our chil'ren like you folks do. We don't ask 'em 'bout colors, names 'n things" stands in stark contrast to the Roadville mother who said:

> I figure it's up to me to give 'im a good start. I reckon there's just some things I know he's gotta learn, you know, what things are, and all that. 'n you just don't happen onto doin' all that right. Now, you take Danny 'n Bobby, we, Betty 'n me, we talk to them kids all the time, like they was grown-up or something, 'n we try to tell 'em 'bout things, 'n books, 'n we buy those educational toys for 'em. (pp. 127-28)

Practices such as these continue until the children in Roadville are about four years old; when they enter school, parents seem to drop their "teaching" practices abruptly, expecting their children to continue their learning in school. Since much of the curriculum in the early school years is similar to the kinds of language practices pre-schoolers experience in Roadville homes, their initial transition to formal schooling is not a difficult one. This, of course, is not the case for the Trackton children, who experience a sharp discontinuity between language practices at home and those at school.

Despite the initial comfortableness of the early elementary schooling routines for the Roadville children, however, they too experience difficulty with formal schooling. This occurs usually in the upper elementary school years, when an increasing emphasis is placed in the school curriculum upon more interpretive and creative uses of language. The reasons for Roadville children's difficulty may lie in the religious beliefs of their community. In Roadville, behavior is seen as either right or wrong, and the belief is that one can learn how to "do right." Being members of a fundamentalist religious community, Roadville adults believe that "right" ways of living can be determined by reference to the Bible, or "the Word." Verses from the Bible are learned verbatim by children at an early age, and are continually referred to in order to retrieve "morals" to live by. Knowledge, then, is seen as finite and definite: life can be understood and dealt with by understanding what is already in the Bible, that is, everything necessary to know is there already.

This belief in what Heath terms "the finite nature of religious knowledge" stands in stark contrast to the emphasis on creative alternatives in Trackton. Though Trackton is also a religious community, the language and other cultural practices are quite different in the two communities. In Trackton churches, for example, a written text (e.g., a prayer or a hymn) is presented orally with many interpretive variations. In Roadville, in contrast, truth is literal, rather than metaphoric. When children socialized into these two communities confront a "new" culture (that of "mainstream" schooling), they are faced, in different ways, with learning vastly different ways of seeing the world and of using language, both oral and written, in that world.

Heath has provided a detailed ethnographic description of two communities whose children generally do not succeed in school. She has shown how the language practices of a particular community or culture are closely tied to the beliefs and conceptual principles by which the people in that community live and that these practices may differ more or less starkly with the language practices of the school community or culture. Since school in our society is generally part of mainstream culture, the language practices in school are also culturally embedded. In other words, school literacy and orality are also closely tied to beliefs and conceptual principles by which a certain group of people live—in this case, what Street (1984) has called the "academic sub-culture" of our society. Here, objectivity and explicitness are valued, especially in written language, and consequently Western schools attempt to teach students how to generate written language that displays these qualities. Thus one typical teacher comment on a student essay is "But why do you think this is so?" When the student writer provides his or her reason orally, the response is often "Good, but you didn't say that here. It's not in the writing."

Instruction in literacy, then, for those students who do not come from mainstream culture, is partially a matter of acculturation to mainstream culture. Many of the difficulties that such students have in succeeding, and becoming literate, in school can be explained by the complexity of the differences between their home culture and the school culture.

It is sometimes tempting to minimize such cultural differences and be frustrated that students don't quickly or easily learn the school's "new" ways of using language. One might argue that, since all children are, by nature, avid learners—after all, they have learned to speak a language mostly through exposure to it over a relatively short period of time—they should be able to adjust to the new context of school relatively easily. The fact that they don't, that schools with mostly nonmainstream students have limited success in literacy instruction, should make it clear that the situation is not a simple one. Cultural differences in language practices that are a part of very different ways of viewing and operating in the world must be taken seriously indeed. They can be both extensive and deeply ingrained, as Heath and many other researchers have shown. As such, they no doubt provide substantial explanation for the difficulties inherent in the teaching of writing to nonstandard-dialect-speaking students.

Linguistic Differences

Purely linguistic explanations (i.e., those due to structural differences between nonstandard dialects and standard English) are another substantial explanation for difficulties in teaching and learning writing. Linguistic explanations may shed some light on why it seems so difficult, even for older, highly motivated composition students, to learn to edit vernacular features out of their writing. We have learned through research that this problem is generally limited to a few frequently occurring nonstandard features (Farr Whiteman 1981a, and others). In addition, we know that in the oral language of such nonstandard-dialect speakers these nonstandard features almost never occur categorically (i.e., 100 percent of the time); they usually alternate with the standard variant of the feature. For example, even the most "true" Vernacular Black English speakers omit the standard plural -*s* suffix (e.g., *many friend-*) only about 30 percent of the time; the rest of the time they include it. This raises a question: if a speaker uses this suffix even occasionally, doesn't he or she in some sense "know" it? And, if this is the case, then why does the nonstandard variant of this feature (i.e., the absence of -*s*) so persistently occur, for example, in school compositions, despite explicit teaching of the standard variant for years?

In addition to the deeply ingrained nature of linguistic rules and the high frequencies of occurrence of some nonstandard features, the inherent variability of particular features probably increases the difficulty of learning to produce standard English features. As we discussed in a preceding section, much of the variation within a dialect is firmly conditioned according to the local linguistic context. For example, some studies (Wolfram and Fasold 1974) have shown that the absence of the -*s* suffix mentioned above may occur more frequently with measure nouns (e.g., *ten cent-*) than with other kinds of nouns. It makes sense that this kind of established conditioning in a person's linguistic competence would be reflected in both oral and written language performance. Such unconscious but highly structured rules unfortunately work against the kind of linguistic shift that is asked for in the more formal registers of language used in the classroom. This points out, once again, how deep-seated and intricately structured all language use is. It also emphasizes the difficulty of using conscious strategies to change largely unconscious processes.

Bidialectalism

For years, many scholars and educators have advocated "bidialectalism" as an educational goal for students whose native language is a nonstandard dialect. This position is based first on the assumption that as linguistic systems, nonstandard dialects are as valid as "standard English" and that they are quite appropriate in certain situations. This assumption has much support from sociolinguistic studies of various nonstandard dialects and from ethnographic studies of language use in various contexts. There is another assumption, however, which does not have such support from research, and it also often underlies the advocacy of bidialectalism. This is the assumption that if one "acquires" a second "dialect," one will have two linguistic systems to call upon in communicating, either orally or in writing.

The concept of bidialectalism was modeled on that of bilingualism. Inasmuch as this analogy implies that a nonstandard dialect is as self-contained a linguistic system as is a more standard variety of a language, it is accurate. Unfortunately, however, this analogy also leads to an oversimplification of what *language,* or even *dialect,* actually means. These are linguistic terms, and they are essentially abstract concepts which refer to a linguistic description of the underlying language system used by a particular group of people. This does not mean that a particular system exists *in toto* and exactly in a particular form in any one speaker's mind; rather, it is a description abstracted from group behavior.

Whether or not two "dialects" (even if we concede that standard English is a dialect), or two languages for that matter, exist as separate systems in the minds of particular speakers is a question that can only be answered empirically. So far the evidence from research is mixed and inconclusive, as has been pointed out by Ferguson (1977):

> Recent studies of very early bilingual development in children (up to about three years of age) give evidence that the children at first have a single linguistic system with elements drawn from both languages, and then gradually differentiate the two by applying "rules" selectively. . . . A striking recent study of phonetic perception and production in many monolingual and bilingual (English and French) Canadians suggests that some bilinguals have two

productive systems corresponding well to those of monolinguals,
but have developed a combined perception system different from
either monolingual system. . . . (p. 49)

Recent research by Labov and his associates (Labov and Harris
1983; Ash and Myhill 1983; Myhill and Harris 1983; Graff, Labov, and
Harris 1983) also provides evidence which leads us to question the
possibility of actual bidialectalism. In their program of research on
lingustic change and variation, they concluded that black and white
dialects in Philadelphia, and quite possibly in the other major
Northern cities, are increasingly diverging. They speculate that this
linguistic behavior is reflective of increasingly segregated societies. If
this is true, the challenge of providing literacy instruction amid such
diversity will become even greater. It may be, in fact, that better field-
work in collecting natural language samples is providing evidence for
a dialect which was always so divergent from standard English. But
whether that is the case, or whether true Vernacular Black English is
in fact becoming more different from white varieties of American
English, we are faced with the same problem in educational terms.

By carefully documenting the social networks of the black and
white speakers they studied, Labov and his associates were able to
relate the occurrence of nonstandard features with patterns of social
interaction, distinguishing two groups of people: those who have
"meaningful contact" with the "opposite" ethnic group, and those
who do not. Ash and Myhill (1983) define "meaningful contact" as
that between

> people who work together, socialize together, live together, and
> generally mean to be fully participating members of an ethnic
> community other than their own. (p. 2)

They conclude that although there is considerable "borrowing" of
vocabulary and phonological (pronunciation) features across ethnic
groups who have meaningful contact with each other, the case is
quite different for grammatical features:

> Blacks who mingle with whites go a long way towards acquiring
> the white norm, but whites who mingle with blacks make very
> little progress toward acquiring the black norm for these vari-
> ables. (p. 13)

The same point is made elsewhere: "Blacks who move in white circles
show a major shift in their grammar in the direction of the white
norm" (p. 16), but the same is not true for whites who move in black
circles. Although such whites can learn to "sound black" by using
black pronunciation and vocabulary, they do not acquire Vernacular

Black English grammar. Such asymmetry is not surprising, considering the social and especially political value of standard English, as opposed to Vernacular Black English, in the mainstream society.

The educational implications of these findings are substantial. Apparently, underlying grammatical patterns of standard English are learned through "meaningful" and intensive interaction with those who already use standard English grammar, not "simply by exposure in the mass media or in schools" (Labov and Harris 1983, p. 22). The researchers go on to state,

> Our basic language system is not acquired from school teachers or from radio announcers, but from friends and competitors: those who we admire, and those we have to be good enough to beat.
>
> In the black community of Philadelphia, the core group remains apart, and is probably drifting further apart, in spite of the fact that members hear standard English dialects spoken four to eight hours a day: on television, radio, and in the schools. On the other hand, those speakers who engage in structured interaction with whites, where they use language to negotiate their position or gain advantages, show a profound shift of their grammatical rules. (p. 23)

It seems clear from the work of Labov and his associates that learning standard English probably does not entail learning a new dialect in addition to one's native dialect, and consequently maintaining two separate linguistic systems. What it seems to entail instead is a substantial shift, or change in one's "home" linguistic system, toward the features of standard English. Such change, moreover, only seems to occur when the learners interact seriously and frequently with standard English speakers. Though these results were obtained in a study of oral language use, it seems reasonable to assume a parallel situation with written language use—with writing and reading.

Learning to write, of course, involves more than learning standard English grammar. The cultural orientations associated with Western literacy are often at odds with the orientations to language and literacy in the nonWestern cultures and nonmainstream subcultures which many students come from. It is nevertheless clear, however, that standard English grammar remains one important goal of literacy instruction in most schools. Moreover, acquiring standard English grammar appears to be an important aspect of "entering the mainstream" and acquiring power. As one of us has argued elsewhere (Farr 1985b),

> Over the last decade or so, increasing numbers of blacks and other minorities have entered a variety of business and professional arenas, from anchoring the news to running for President. All of

them publicly use a very "standard" English, at least in grammatical terms. Although other aspects of their language use (pronunciation, intonation, vocabulary) may at times reflect regional
and ethnic characteristics, their grammar is standard. They may
retain aspects of their cultural and linguistic heritages for use in
other contexts, but they certainly know how to use standard
English so as to be taken seriously by those in power. (p. 109)

This does not mean, of course, that we should continue to teach
grammar the way it has generally been taught for decades. In fact,
Labov's results indicate that more emphasis should be placed in
school on "meaningful interaction" with written language, and not
on workbook exercises isolated from a meaningful context. In the
next chapter, we will consider in more detail the issues involved in
making changes in the classroom, including those which deal with
the teaching of grammar. Before moving to pedagogical issues, however, it is necessary to explore further the relations among the dialects
of a language, particularly between a nonstandard one and the "standard" one being taught in school.

"Dialect Interference": Conflict between Communicative Systems

The term "dialect interference in writing" was first used (Wolfram
and Whiteman 1971) to refer to the use of nonstandard-dialect features
in written compositions. This usage was based on the assumption
that the writer, though a native speaker of a nonstandard dialect,
intended to write in standard English. The term was created as a
parallel to the "language interference" that sometimes occurs in the
speech of bilinguals. That is, when a person knows two languages,
sometimes features from one language will occur when that person is
speaking the other language. For example, native French speakers
will often use a z sound instead of the voiced *th* sound in words such as
this or *that*. In this case of language interference, the pronunciation
system of French is "interfering" with the pronunciation of English.
    The concept of dialect interference only has validity if we assume
that two linguistic systems (or dialects) exist separately (rather than as
one system, with variation built in) in the mind of the speaker/writer.
We now know that this is doubtful, as we have seen in the preceding
section on bidialectalism. Thus, the term can only be useful if we use
it to mean a conflict between different linguistic systems, and if we
remember that "dialect" actually means *a linguistic description that
has been abstracted from the language behavior of a particular group.*
Generally speaking, members of the group do have this system as

their native dialect; that is, they share many of the linguistic rules of the dialect. Because these rules differ in some respects from those of standard English, nonstandard-dialect speakers will encounter some difficulty when expected to use the standard dialect in school. Furthermore, if and when they begin to assimilate rules of standard English, their own linguistic systems will begin to change and shift toward the standard.

Such a shift toward standard English, of course, does not always occur. Many students who come from nonmainstream cultures learn neither standard English grammar nor other aspects of writing which enable them to "write well." The problem of conflict between different communicative systems is worth considering in some detail because of its importance in explaining educational difficulties. To explore the possibilities for conflict, we will use a conceptual framework comprising five broad domains of language, and we will provide an example of conflict between standard and nonstandard ways of communicating in each domain.

There are five broad domains of language comprising what a speaker knows about the communicative system of his or her culture. Although linguists disagree about how these domains are grouped and organized to represent a native speaker's linguistic knowledge, they agree that these domains exist in some form. That is, all people who speak a language, or a dialect of a language, have these five domains as part of their overall language competence. The domains are:

1. Phonology (rules of pronunciation)
2. Syntax (rules of morphology and word order)
3. Semantics (meanings associated with grammar, vocabulary, and patterns of discourse)
4. Pragmatics (rules of use)
5. Discourse (patterns of language beyond the sentence)

Phonology consists of the rules for pronouncing the words of a language. The differences among regional dialects in the United States are due largely to differences in phonology, or pronunciation. For example, southerners and New Englanders often omit -*r* sounds that occur after vowels (e.g., in *park, car, mother*, etc.). Should a student who pronounces words like these without the postvocalic -*r* also write the word without an *r*, then this would be a case of dialect interference. In addition to regional dialects, some social dialects differ from standard English in parts of their phonology. For example, it is common for Vernacular Black English speakers to omit the final member of a consonant cluster at the ends of certain words (e.g., *closes'*, rather than *closest*). Sometimes, then, a VBE speaker will write such words without the final consonant; this, again, is an example of dialect interference. Although phonological dialect influence doesn't occur as frequently as other kinds of dialect influence (Farr Whiteman 1981a), it does occur regularly in the compositions of students who speak nonstandard dialects.

Syntax is that part of linguistic knowledge which allows a speaker to put words in the appropriate order to make sentences in a language. In the United States, the differences between various social dialects and standard English often are the result of differences in syntactic rules. For example, according to the rules of Vernacular Black English, the possessive *-s* suffix may be used, but it doesn't have to be. Thus if a VBE-speaking student writes *My friend car,* that is probably the result of dialect interference. Recent research has shown that, in addition to inflections (such as *-s*), there are a number of differences between standard English and VBE in the verb tense and aspect system (e.g., in the use of the VBE *be, been, done,* and other features). Although many of the special features which mark the VBE tense and aspect system occur only rarely and in "vernacular" settings, they occasionally appear in writing. For example, in an essay arguing against smoking, one student wrote *They be smoking on the butt of the thing* (Farr and Janda 1985). For a cogent and clear description of the distinctive tense-aspect features of VBE, see Labov (1983).

The third domain of language listed above, semantics, deals with the meanings represented by words, sentences, and discourse patterns. Although there hasn't been much research on differences in semantic systems among dialects, there are both clearly distinguished and more subtle differences between standard English and various nonstandard dialects. Sometimes a word or a phrase is used to convey a meaning that is entirely different from the meaning conveyed in standard English (e.g., the use of *broom* to mean "fast getaway," as in *I don't have a car so I think I'll broom;* Kochman 1972a). Other times, a word may be used similarly to standard English but with an added negative or positive feature (e.g., the use of the word *attitude* in VBE to mean "a negative attitude," as in *That woman has an attitude*). According to Kochman's (1972a) analysis, meanings in the semantic system of VBE are closely linked to the cultural norms of that community, and a variety of usages often cohere around themes reflecting these norms (he explores the themes of movement, contest, and control). For an extensive description of culturally specific expressive uses of Black English, see all the essays in Kochman 1972b.

Pragmatics, the fourth domain of language, deals with the use of language in context. Some definitions of pragmatics focus on how the "literal" meaning of an utterance changes according to factors in the context of the utterance (e.g., the setting, the participants, their roles, what has occurred previously in the discourse, etc.). Other definitions focus on appropriateness: "Pragmatics is the study of the ability of language users to pair sentences with the contexts in which they would be appropriate" (Levinson 1983, p. 24). For example, Levinson (1983, p. 43) uses the following two sentences to indicate differing levels of politeness, each of which would be appropriate in different contexts:

1. I want to see you for a moment.

2. I wondered if I could possibly see you for a moment.

Pragmatics also differentiates between the *form* of an utterance and its *function*. For example, in a particular context an utterance which takes the form of a question can actually function as a directive: a teacher, noticing a student wandering around the room, might ask, "Have you finished your math?"—meaning "Sit down and finish your math." Thus an interrogative can actually be intended, and interpreted, as a directive. It is not difficult to interpret the intended meaning of such an utterance if the speaker and hearer share the same cultural background; however, differences across cultures can lend complexity to this process, with misunderstanding and even conflict the result.

Philips's (1972, 1983) account of the language use of American Indian children at home and at school provides an example of the difficulty of cross-cultural communication, even when the same language is being used. In this study Indian and Anglo children systematically responded differently to the teacher's imperatives and interrogatives, depending upon what Philips termed the "participant structures" in the classroom. Philips identified four participant structures: the whole class in interaction with the teacher, a small group in interaction with the teacher, one-to-one involvement between the teacher and a single student, and "desk work" (when a student's attention is focused on written materials on his or her desk). The first three structures influence the way verbal interaction is structured in the classroom; the latter, of course, does not involve such interaction.

Depending upon the participant structure being used, the Indian children often were silent in response to teacher questions and did not comply with teacher directives. Philips was able to determine that this occurred not because they did not understand the linguistic structure of the interrogative or the imperative, but "because they [did] not share the non-Indian's assumption in such contexts that use of these syntactic forms by definition implies an automatic and immediate response from the person to whom they were addressed" (1972, p. 392). These Indian children were perceived to be "non-comprehending" by many Anglo teachers because of such lack of response in certain classroom situations. Philips's ethnographic study, however, because it contrasted patterns of language use at home and at school, illuminated the reasons for this characteristic lack of immediate response.

In communicative contexts which resembled those characteristic of language use at home, the children responded. In the classroom, however, the "absence of the appropriate social conditions for communicative performances" accounted for the frequent lack of response by the Indian children (Philips 1972, p. 392). This and other such studies have shown us that the same linguistic form (for example, a question) actually is used very differently in various contexts by different cultural groups—a fact which accounts for much miscommunication between people from different cultural backgrounds.

Although this example deals with oral language use and does not bear directly on writing, it is nevertheless an important example of how the communicative systems with which people unconsciously operate may conflict and thus interfere with all teaching and learning processes in the classroom. Moreover, it is not difficult to conceive of ways in which such conflicts might interfere with learning to write. For example, students who come from cultures in which it is inappropriate for individuals either to speak or to write as a solitary activity, without interaction with an audience (as was the case with the Trackton community in Heath's study), might find it strange and awkward to write in solitary contexts in school. For such students, the interactive use of computers for writing might be a more effective instructional strategy.

The final domain of language we will discuss here is discourse, which refers to language patterns that extend over more than one sentence or utterance. Some studies of discourse have focused on the "rules" by which people unconsciously operate when engaging in conversation (e.g., the rules for turn-taking). Other studies of discourse have focused on the relations among sentences that cohere to comprise a "text," either oral or written. A "text" in this sense is a group of sentences that form a unified whole, rather than being simply a group of unrelated sentences (Halliday and Hasan 1976). Inter-sentence coherence in student compositions is a major concern of most teachers of writing, so it is fortunate that recent research has shown that apparent differences in the degree of such coherence can sometimes be traced to cultural differences in communicative systems.

In several studies of "Sharing Time" (or "Show and Tell") in various elementary school classrooms (Michaels 1981; Michaels and Collins 1984; Cazden, Michaels, and Tabors 1985), Michaels has identified two oral discourse patterns used in narration. One of these patterns, which she termed "topic-centered," is typically used by standard-English-speaking, "mainstream" children. The other pattern, which she termed "topic-associating," is typically used by VBE-speaking inner-city children. Upon close analysis, she found that both patterns evidenced topic cohesion through the narrative, but that the topic-centered pattern showed the cohesion more explicitly by using lexical and syntactic devices (i.e., through explicit vocabulary and grammatical connectives). This type of pattern, though evidenced orally in this common classroom speech event, is close to what is expected in school literacy—it is, in fact, the kind of pattern we teach students to use when writing. Because of this match, students who "know" and use this oral discourse pattern before coming to school probably have an easier transition to the formal teaching and learning of writing in school.

Those students who unconsciously know and use, as part of their native communication system, other discourse patterns which do not match the school's model of literacy presumably have a much more difficult transition to make. For example, in the topic-associating pattern, topics are implicitly connected through intonation contours rather than with explicit vocabulary and connectives (e.g., *then* or *so*, rather than *and*). Other researchers have referred to a similar discourse style among black Americans. Smitherman (1977) describes black adult narrative style as "concrete narrative . . . [whose] meandering away from the point takes the listener on episodic journeys" (pp. 147–48). In addition, Erickson (1984), in a study of black adolescents informally discussing politics, found that shifts from one topic to another were not explicitly stated. Rather, meanings had to be inferred from a series of concrete anecdotes. Although this style of discourse can be difficult to follow for those who are not part of this cultural group, close analysis reveals "a most rigorous logic and a systematic coherence of the particular, whose internal system is organized not by literate style linear sequentiality but by audience/speaker interaction" (p. 152).

The above descriptions by Michaels, Smitherman, and Erickson affirm the results of other studies of black American speech, which describe it as culturally different from, but not deficient in comparison to, mainstream uses of both oral language and literacy. The advantage that mainstream speakers have, of course, is that school literacy is modeled on their own uses of language.

Conclusion

We have provided in this chapter an extensive review of what research so far has shown about the use of, and the capacities for, language by native nonstandard speakers of English. The research base is far from complete: though phonology and syntax have been explored for a few nonmainstream groups, there is a paucity of information about the other language domains (semantics, pragmatics, and discourse) for more than a few nonmainstream groups. Moreover, it is these latter domains, and particularly the discourse domain, which may have the most relevance for application to the teaching of (mainstream) extended expository text.

In spite of the limitations of research-based knowledge in this area, we have provided detailed explanations of what we do know from such research. We have done so because we believe an understanding of the language capacities of nonmainstream students is crucial to a teacher's effectiveness in facilitating such students' acquisition of literacy. We believe it is crucial for two primary reasons: first, learning to use written language shares a common language base with learning to use oral language; consequently, the teaching of literacy must be founded, among other things, on a substantial understanding of the nature of human language.

Second, we believe that in order for any kind of teaching to be effective, teachers must understand as fully as possible the resources their students bring with them to school. Utilizing and building on these resources are the keys to teaching writing to nonmainstream students. The next chapter addresses what research on writing instruction has shown us about the effective teaching of writing, both to mainstream and nonmainstream students. We will also present some specific classroom practices derived from this research.

3 Writing Instruction and Nonmainstream Students

During the past two decades a substantial literature on writing and the teaching of writing has developed. So many research studies, theoretical works, and program reports have been completed during this period that we can now point to a number of key practices consistently associated with improvement in student writing performance. Unfortunately, little of this research has been done with the nonmainstream adolescents we are particularly concerned with here. However, we are confident that this more general research on writing instruction, when viewed through the perspective of the linguistic principles we have just outlined, can offer valuable guidance to teachers of nonmainstream students.

As we stressed early in Chapter 2, the speakers of all languages and dialects employ the same fundamental linguistic processes and capabilities. Given this principle, there is no reason to believe that the task of learning to write is different in *kind* for a student who speaks a nonstandard, as opposed to a prestige, dialect of English. Therefore, we approach the general research on writing instruction with the assumption that, in the absence of specific indications to the contrary, the teaching of writing to students from *all* linguistic backgrounds may be guided by the general principles that emerge from the research on composition. Just as the linguistic rules underlying the dialects customarily labeled "standard" and "nonstandard" mostly overlap (as illustrated by Wolfram and Fasold's circle diagram in Chapter 2), so we expect that the rules underlying good composition pedagogy will mostly overlap, even for students with widely varying linguistic backgrounds.

However, this does not mean that writing instruction in ethnic urban and other linguistically nonmainstream schools can or should be identical to that offered in linguistically homogenous, mainstream suburban high schools. On the contrary, there need to be significant differences. Our knowledge of the best available practices needs to be translated, adapted, and rearranged to fit the special needs of nonmainstream students and the conditions of the schools they attend.

Indeed, the rest of this book is primarily concerned with making these adjustments. However, in addressing this task, we recognize that such adjustments are not differences of kind.

In adapting promising teaching practices to nonmainstream students, there is one special danger: focusing mainly on the problem of error. This understandable temptation must be resisted for a number of reasons. Nonmainstream students are, of course, likely to produce a great number of grammatical and mechanical errors in their written work, many of which may stem from the influence of their spoken language. The writing of these students, in other words, may contain an extra measure of errors in the form of stigmatized features from their oral dialect that don't match the official language of school or the preferred language of academic writing. The appearance of these features in writing, sometimes in great quantity, may lure us into the mistaken belief that the main problem these students face in learning to write is their divergence from the standard dialect, when in fact the even greater challenge—the same one faced by all pupils in school—is learning how to make sense on paper. As Mina Shaughnessy has said, "[These] students write the way they do, not because they are slow or non-verbal, indifferent to or incapable of academic excellence, but because they are beginners" (1977, p. 5).

While most writing teachers would undoubtedly endorse Shaughnessy's sympathetic view of their students' predicament, they also feel a strong professional obligation to attend closely to students' errors. And if certain students produce a great many errors, such attention can occupy a great deal—or even all—of the available class time. As we will shortly review, however, the existing research on composition pedagogy offers little support for the idea of making error, or grammatical and usage issues, the main focus of composition instruction. On the contrary, such practices have consistently been among the least effective alternatives, and have been associated with no growth or actual regression in student writing performance (Hillocks 1986). To put it bluntly, then, there is no reason that an approach to writing that has failed with mainstream students should be made the center of the curriculum for nonmainstream students, unless we have conclusive evidence that it will work.

There is one other set of assumptions that needs to be reviewed before we move on to the research and its implications. In this book, we are mainly concerned with high school students who are native speakers of nonstandard English. What assumptions have we made about the writing instruction that these students have received prior to arriving in high school? Generally, we assume that they have had the same kind of background in writing that most American elementary students experience: a poor one. As the National Assessment of Educational Progress has shown, only about 7 percent of American schoolchildren overall are receiving the kind of thorough instruction in writing that leads to facility and fluency (NAEP 1981, Applebee 1986). Probably nonmainstream students actually have a somewhat weaker preparation, since many of them attend inner-city elementary schools, which have a generally weak record in literacy education. Nor can many of these students count on out-of-school experiences to compensate for the shortcomings of their schooling; in their homes, families, and communities, they may have fewer literacy resources to draw upon than students from mainstream backgrounds.

Principles from Research and Implications for Teaching

Recent research has enabled us to isolate fifteen key factors associated with effective writing instruction:

1. Teachers who understand and appreciate the basic linguistic competence that students bring with them to school, and who therefore have positive expectations for students' achievements in writing.

2. Regular and substantial practice in writing, aimed at developing fluency.

3. The opportunity to write for real, personally significant purposes.

4. Experience in writing for a wide range of audiences, both inside and outside of school.

5. Rich and continuous reading experience, including both published literature of acknowledged merit and the work of peers and instructors.

6. Exposure to models of writing in process and writers at work, including both teachers and classmates.

7. Instruction in the processes of writing; that is, learning to work at a given writing task in appropriate phases, including prewriting, drafting, and revising.

8. Collaborative activities for students that provide ideas for writing and guidance for revising works in progress.

9. One-to-one writing conferences with the teacher.

10. Direct instruction in specific strategies and techniques for writing.

11. Reduced instruction in grammatical terminology and related drills, with increased use of sentence combining activities.

12. Teaching of writing mechanics and grammar in the context of students' actual compositions, rather than in separate drills or exercises.

13. Moderate marking of surface structure errors, focusing on sets or patterns of related errors.

14. Flexible and cumulative evaluation of student writing that stresses revision and is sensitive to variations in subject, audience, and purpose.

15. Practicing and using writing as a tool of learning in all subjects in the curriculum, not just in English.

In the remainder of this section, we will discuss how each of the above factors may connect with the needs of high school students who are native speakers of nonstandard forms of English. For each of these principles, we touch upon two main aspects. First, we briefly outline some of the research studies that lend support to the pedagogical principle under consideration. We have stressed empirical findings where they are available and have cited program reports or theoretical works where empirical confirmation is not available or has not been attempted. Since we are primarily concerned with high school students, we have emphasized studies done at that level, but in this relatively young field of composition research one must also examine a variety of related studies, translating results up and down the ages. While we believe it is helpful to treat the fifteen principles on our list separately, some of them have been investigated only in combination with other practices, and have not been fully confirmed as discrete strategies.

For the second part of our presentation on each principle, we turn to instructional issues, comparing current classroom practice with the methods suggested by research. We have tried to show the connections between the linguistic knowledge outlined in Chapter 2 and each practice under review here. Some of these teaching ideas need considerable adjustment to work well with nonmainstream students, while others can be applied more or less identically to all students. One thing the research has consistently shown, and George Hillocks (1986) has explicated, is that the most powerful instructional programs in writing use a combination of the techniques outlined below.

While it is certainly not necessary—nor even possible—for a school to fully implement every one of these fifteen ideas, there seems to be a synergistic effect when several are intertwined. This means, of course, that the potential number of effective instructional designs and sequences of activities is countless. Therefore, in this section we can only offer broad pedagogical suggestions with a few specific examples. Teachers who desire more detailed guidance on specific practices may consult some of the practitioner-oriented resources listed in our bibliography.

As we set out to offer suggestions to teachers, we are mindful of the tremendous variety of pupils with whom they work. Some of these students are sprinkled in predominantly mainstream classrooms; others go to school amidst a heterogenous variety of standard-English speakers and various linguistic minorities; still others go to schools where their own nonstandard dialect is spoken by all the students. And though it is certainly not the predominant pattern, some of these students, especially those who belong to economically disadvantaged racial minorities, attend schools where there may be true alienation or chaos: where no one, teacher nor student, can really concentrate on learning because their psychic or even physical safety is in constant and pressing danger.

For teachers who work in such troubled schools, much of what we are about to propose will sound naive and idealistic. We sympathize with them and hope they may find in this book an idea or two that *will* work in their setting, that can begin to create something hopeful and valuable in their difficult conditions. Meanwhile, for the rest—the majority—of teachers working with these students, in schools where learning goes on every day and where teachers have the confidence and autonomy to innovate, we offer the following.

1. Teachers who understand and appreciate the basic linguistic competence that students bring with them to school, and who therefore have positive expectations for students' achievements in writing.

The power of teacher attitudes in determining the outcomes of various educational programs has long been recognized (Rosenthal and Jacobsen 1968). We have just recently begun to confirm that teacher attitudes and expectations have the same power to affect the results of writing instruction.

In their four-year study of writing teachers at work, Perl and Wilson (1986) found that the most basic distinction between successful and unsuccessful instructors was their attitude toward their students.

According to Perl, the effective writing teachers viewed their students as bringing considerable linguistic skill to the task of learning to write. These teachers saw students as linguistically competent and described their own task as one of helping the student along to the next stage in a continuous process of language development. The less effective teachers, on the other hand, were more likely to view their students' language as being underdeveloped or deficient; they tended not to give their students as much credit for being able to use language effectively on their own terms. Significantly, Perl found that when teachers held the second set of attitudes—viewing students as linguistically inadequate—their classroom use of even the most exemplary, research-validated teaching methods still failed to achieve the expected growth in students' performance.

Perl's findings explain why we place teacher expectations at the top of our list of principles for effective writing instruction. Indeed, if even the best available teaching methods can fail when implemented by teachers who lack a genuine, fundamental appreciation for what students can already do with language, then no insight can be more important to those of us considering improvements in the teaching of writing. Unfortunately, students who speak one of the nonstandard forms of English—whether a black urban dialect, Spanish-influenced English, or a rural variety—don't always encounter teachers with such positive, nurturing attitudes toward the language pupils bring to school. On the contrary, some teachers may take a quite negative, even punitive approach toward nonstandard dialects, which they may even disparage as "street talk."

After two decades of linguistic study of nonstandard dialects—much of which we just reviewed in Chapter 2—and the dissemination of the findings to the schools, some teachers still actively discourage or attack students' use of any vernacular that doesn't match the official dialect of the school. It is still not uncommon for teachers to pretend that they don't understand an utterance that's offered in a nonstandard form ("I don't got no money." "Oh, so you *do* have some money, then.") These and similar strategies are justified as attempts to force students to adopt a preferred dialect in oral or written work, and have been shown to be pedagogically ineffective (Daniels 1973). Usually, these teachers mean well, and they are not necessarily ethnocentric Anglos; many have themselves been native speakers of a stigmatized dialect and may be enacting a strong personal commitment to help others escape the vernacular, as they believe they have.

Why do so many teachers feel and act so negatively toward the home language of children they otherwise treat with respect? To begin with, teachers are influenced by many of the same social attitudes that exist among the general population, prejudices that devalue and ridicule nonstandard forms of English. Beyond this, American school teachers also have a strong professional tradition as guardians of the genteel culture, especially as it is reflected in polite, standard language. Every school teacher—not just those specifically assigned to teach English and language arts—feels some sense of duty to uphold correctness in speech and writing. After all, we still send our children to "grammar schools," and even if the origins of the name aren't directly related to standard English, the idea of propriety in speech is still firmly rooted in American public education and in the professional culture of its teachers (Heath 1980, Drake 1974).

The point is that teachers are likely to have language attitudes that are both very strong and very negative toward the nonstandard dialects some students bring to school (Williams 1976). And as these students take up the considerable challenge of learning to write, they need to have their fundamental capacities as human language users affirmed, supported, and appreciated—not denigrated. Nonmainstream students need to have a relationship with the kind of writing teacher Perl describes: a person who recognizes that the pupil arrives in English class as a rather accomplished user of language, and who views the main task as helping the student along toward the next stage of linguistic growth.

If this kind of relationship is so rare and yet so vital to creating an effective writing program for nonmainstream students, how can it be nurtured? Obviously there is a considerable job of teacher training involved here. Both preservice and inservice teachers should be exposed to the research on language variation, and they also should develop (or be helped to develop) a descriptive understanding of any nonstandard dialects used by the students they teach. Chapter 2 of this book, for example, contains some of the linguistic information that we believe teachers need as a foundation for working with students from nonmainstream backgrounds. Whatever materials they study, teachers must at least comprehend, both intellectually and affectively, that all dialects, regardless of their social valuation, are logical, rule-governed systems capable of carrying any human meanings their speakers may intend. Equally important, teachers need to develop the habit of immersing themselves in the natural and spontaneous language which their students use, absorbing its sound, structures, values, and styles. Teachers need to develop a nonjudgmental, descriptive "ear" for their students' dialects, becoming able to recognize what the students can do with language.

While we realize that organized training can help teachers develop these understandings and approaches, we have no illusion that mere training will quickly or completely eliminate negative attitudes. Information is a notoriously weak treatment when it comes to shaping or changing something so powerful as language attitudes. Experts who have tried to develop training programs to alter linguistic prejudices have testified to the difficulty of the task (Burling 1970). Even with an exemplary teacher-training program, one that provides for active exploration of language attitudes as well as information about linguistic realities, many teachers will still need a great deal of time and much direct experience with students before they begin to exhibit truly understanding and accepting attitudes toward nonstandard dialects.

We realize that the institution-wide attitude changes we've called for will not come to pass in many schools. But individual teachers can learn and can change their behavior in the classroom. Even in a school system where the official policy toward nonstandard dialects is unenlightened and punitive, a knowledgeable, caring teacher can not only moderate the impact of such institutional discouragement, but may even create a linguistic safe harbor, a climate of understanding and encouragement in his or her own room. For students whose school experience feels like a continuous buffeting of rejection, this interlude of acceptance may be tremendously powerful.

2. *Regular and substantial practice in writing, aimed at developing fluency.*

As noted in Chapter 1, one of the critical deficiencies in present-day writing instruction is students' sheer lack of writing practice. As the findings of Applebee (1981) and the National Assessment of Educational Progress (1981) demonstrate, only a tiny fraction of American students at any age level are writing enough, by NAEP's or any other reasonable standard, to become proficient. About half of the high school students in this country are asked to write a paragraph or more only twice a year or less; the average student still writes an essay or report of a paragraph about every other week. It is simply inconceivable that students who write so little could become effective writers, any more than one could become skilled at any complex activity—be it bricklaying, piano playing, or race-car driving—without more than brief semiannual practice sessions.

Writing practice is important in several ways. To begin with, experience with writing can build familiarity and comfort, leading to the relatively fluent production of written language (Moffet 1968).

More significantly, students need writing practice because writing, like other aspects of human language, is best learned in actual use, rather than in decontextualized exercises or drills (Falk 1979, Britton 1970).

Unfortunately, the necessity for practice in writing has been obscured by the misunderstanding of several widely cited studies. The research of Heys (1962), Arnold (1963), and Christensen (1967), which showed no gains for students writing frequently over others writing less often, has appeared prominently in summaries of research directed at elementary and secondary teachers (Haynes 1978, California State Dept. of Education 1982). Most of these studies, however, were conducted in settings where both treatment and experimental groups were doing a substantial amount of writing (often in college composition courses), and the essential contrast was not between little writing and a lot, but between a good deal of writing and (according to the results) too much. In other words, these studies offer no endorsement to schools where students write one or two paragraphs a year. They only show that there is a level of practice—which most American high schools do not even distantly approach—beyond which the sheer volume of writing becomes less valuable than the more careful development, over time, of a smaller body of written work.

For nonmainstream students, lack of practice may be an especially serious handicap. Mina Shaughnessy, whose *Errors and Expectations* is one of the most widely cited works on teaching writing to minority students, has insisted that the fundamental problem of these students, whom she calls "basic writers," is less their culture or their oral dialect than their catastrophic lack of experience in writing: "Compared with the 1000 words a week that a British student is likely to have written in the equivalent of an American high school or even the 350 words a week that an American student in a middle-class high school is likely to have written, the basic writing student is more likely to have written 350 words a semester. It would not be unusual for him to have written nothing at all" (1977, p. 14).

Not only have these students written infrequently, but often their few efforts with extended written discourse have been treated in a way that discourages future writing. As Shaughnessy recounts this pattern of discouragement, "For the [nonmainstream] student, academic writing is a trap, not a way of saying something to someone. . . . [W]riting is but a line that moves haltingly across the page, exposing as it goes all that the writer doesn't know, then passing into the hands of a stranger who reads it with a lawyer's eyes, searching for flaws" (1977, p. 7).

Other factors may undercut opportunities for writing practice for these students. When schools serve many students from economic, social, or linguistic minorities, the curriculum is often reorganized to make learning more segmented, subdivided, and decontextualized; this is called "skill-building." The assumption is that if students do not bring middle-class language and learning styles with them to the classroom, the presumed subcomponents of these "skills" need to be taught to the children first, before anything else can be learned. In practice, this means that students spend a good deal of time working on oral drills and workbook pages that have no immediate meaning or application. On the other hand, students from more favored backgrounds more often engage in activities that are meaningful and holistic, and they get somewhat more practice with writing as they move through school (King and Rentel 1981). While there is certainly not enough writing practice for these students either, they at least have some opportunity to engage in activities that contain interrelated experience in reading, writing, speaking, and listening.

Clearly, the issue of practice is related to the attitude problems raised earlier. If teachers and school officials believe that nonmainstream students cannot use language effectively when they arrive at high school, then it seems logical to them to teach subcomponents of language skills. But once one understands that the students are accomplished language users on their own terms, the justification for "skill building"—especially as the starting point of a writing program—evaporates. Instead, what these students need is the opportunity to practice writing frequently, in a supportive climate, using whatever language they may call upon to get words on paper.

We take our principle here from James Britton (1970), among others: human beings must feel safe to share talk or writing before we can expect them to shape what they have said or written. This is especially the case for students who have lacked practice with written language and who have become accustomed to having their vernacular criticized by outsiders: they must first develop confidence in themselves as writers. Therefore, the first instructional goal in a writing program for such students must be fluency: the relatively free, comfortable, and copious production of written discourse on subjects of real meaning and importance—without penalty for the forms of language used.

Developing fluency takes time. Because of students' poor school experience, and also because home conditions may not be conducive to writing practice, the writing teacher must allow for significant and regular writing time in class. For high school English students, one full period per week of in-class writing is certainly appropriate, and such an arrangement also provides a structure the teacher can use for several of the other activities described below. Some teachers may find it more useful to set aside a shorter period of writing time during every class period, perhaps the first ten minutes of each day's session. However the writing is scheduled, we emphasize that this use of class time to build fluency is a starting point, a strategy to create a productive atmosphere and positive habits, and is not meant to be the permanent focus of the class. Later, when students have gained confidence and productivity, the work can shift toward issues of shaping: revising the meaning and form of drafts, stretching into new modes of discourse. But even though the focus on fluency has been temporary, this doesn't mean it has been a one-time-only remediation of past difficulties. This special kind of writing practice may need to be used over and over, perhaps cyclically throughout the curriculum, as students move along to different teachers and courses. Above all, the students' confidence in their own ability to make meaning with written language needs to be sustained as new and more sophisticated demands are made upon that ability.

3. The opportunity to write for real, personally significant purposes.

American high school students have a pencil in their hands for about one-half of the school day, but during only 3 percent of that time are they writing anything as long as a paragraph (Applebee 1981). Obviously, writing in school is harnessed to many small purposes: filling in blanks, answering test questions, labeling diagrams, blackening circles on standardized exams, and so forth. Of the little extended writing actually done in most schools, far too much is done for purposes that compromise, rather than enhance, the likelihood that students will grow in power as writers.

It is possible to describe six main purposes to which writing may be put in schools:

1. Writing to show learning
2. Writing to master the conventions of writing
3. Writing to learn
4. Writing to communicate
5. Writing to express the self
6. Writing to create

As James Britton (1975) has shown and others have confirmed (NAEP 1981, Applebee 1981), the vast majority of school writing tasks fall into the first two categories: writing that is assigned mainly to check up on students' learning of subject matter content, and writing to display their mastery of the surface-level conventions of written discourse. Though we have no separate data on the school writing tasks undertaken by students from nonmainstream cultural groups, their opportunities for meaningful writing are probably no more frequent, and may well be scarcer, than for mainstream students.

Typical school writing tasks are not conducive to significant and long-term growth for a number of reasons. The superficiality, sometimes even the falseness, of using writing as a mere check on other assignments undercuts the significance of learning to write for other purposes. After all, writing to think and learn, to explore and express the self, to create aesthetically with language, and to get things accomplished in the world are all vital reasons for using writing, and offer potentially powerful motivation for striving to master them (Mayher, Lester, and Pradl 1983).

School writing that instead stresses the first two purposes often presents writing to students as another hurdle on the long track of schoolish trivialities. These kinds of writing leave few genuine tasks, too little autonomy and responsibility for the writer; there is no real exploration, no real meaning to be made or communicated. Writing may become an empty exercise, what Britton calls a "dummy run." Why should students want to develop this school skill called writing? Indeed, why should they even believe teachers who talk of the glorious intellectual power that accrues to practiced writers when their own experience of it is so superficial and pedestrian?

Where school programs have stressed writing for a broad range of real purposes, students' writing skills have shown substantial growth. Stallard (1974) and Sawkins (1971) found that high school writers classified as successful were much more likely than unsuccessful writers to report conscious awareness of purpose while working on writing assignments. In his meta-analysis of studies on the teaching of writing, George Hillocks (1986) found that one of the basic characteristics of successful writing programs was their use of "writing-to-learn" activities that engage students in purpose-explicit exploratory problem solving. Such programs showed four times as much growth in the general quality of student writing compared to the traditional presentational (teacher-dominated) mode.

If we are ever to convince students of the value of mastering writing, we must prove to them that it is a useful activity, not just another school obedience game. In other words, we need to help these students find writing valuable in accomplishing purposes that they, not just a teacher, define as meaningful. To begin with, this means students must exercise some choice of topics in writing. What Donald Graves (1983) has shown to be true for middle-class New Hampshire elementary school children seems even more necessary for high school students from nonmainstream groups: they need to develop a sense of control, authorship, and ownership in working at writing.

In practice, this means that students entering a new course should frequently be encouraged to develop their own topics, especially during the initial period of practice for fluency that we recommended above. This freedom of choice has both an individual significance and a group significance. For each pupil, it offers a chance to write about things that matter; writing may seem worth the struggle when there is personal investment in the content. And as Graves has pointed out, when the teacher reads, accepts, and responds to the content of what a student has chosen to write, he or she is building a trusting personal relationship that can help sustain the student's commitment to writing.

Some student control of writing activities is also important at the group level. For writers from nonmainstream backgrounds, some of the work they produce when given such free choice may derive from the unique linguistic traditions of their group. Allowing such choice is a positive way of inviting overlap between school activities and home values. Some scholars have argued that bringing these distinctive linguistic traditions into the classroom (e.g., among black Americans, sounding, rapping, playing the dozens) is a vital step not just toward helping students develop as writers but also toward helping them to master the unique rhetorical resources their own cultural traditions offer (Smitherman 1977). Every group of nonmainstream speakers has its own verbal style and culturally distinctive ways of using language that, as shown in Chapter 2, linguists have begun to describe. For now, since we lack complete descriptions for all groups represented in our schools, we can only build our curriculum on a general respect for the diversity of language all children bring to school, and make room in the curriculum for the unique features of each group's verbal style to manifest itself in the students' talk and writing. In this manner, we will find the ways in which these linguistic resources can be integrated into the more formal registers of language use that schools have a responsibility to teach.

Offering students the chance to select their own writing topics may not be so simple, however, since many adolescents have become highly dependent upon teacher direction and don't necessarily welcome such freedom. Students who feel that they have previously failed at writing may be very wary of exposing their personal writings to "a lawyer's eyes." Instead, the initial reaction of many students to a free choice of subjects may be a world-weary plea: "Look, teacher, just tell me exactly what to write, when to write it, how long it's supposed to be, when it's due, and how much the grade is worth."

Inviting students' engagement (and vulnerability) by encouraging them to write about personally significant topics may raise a special challenge for students from poor, inner-city neighborhoods. As one Chicago student patiently explained to her writing teacher, "Around here, you don't see a lot of problems solved by not being tough. You don't like people to know that you need help. It's the toughness and reserve that gets the kid through the day." Thoughtful teachers are sensitive to this reserve, this well-earned caution, and realize that they must prove their own trustworthiness first by creating a safe atmosphere in the classroom. Students may have to be gradually led toward deepening personal engagement with writing topics, with the teacher offering them steadily increasing levels of authority as their comfort and confidence increase. This may mean that the teacher initially will provide several choices of writing assignments for students who are stuck or uncomfortable, or encourage students to discuss possible topics with each other. But whatever direction the teacher provides, he or she should always seek to turn authorship back to the students. Since the objective is for students to find writing useful for their own purposes, the teacher should constantly challenge each writer to take more and more responsibility for the work.

One special way in which a teacher can help provide meaningful writing experience for linguistically divergent students is to engage them in the exchange of journals. A study by Staton (1982 and Staton et al. in press) showed that when a classroom teacher working with minority students maintained a program of "dialogue journals," in which the students and the teacher wrote back and forth on subjects of personal interest without any particular focus on correctness, students' writing skill improved significantly. This and similar classroom strategies provide students a dramatic demonstration that they can successfully communicate with writing.

Yet personal narrative cannot be the only purpose to which writing is put in school. After all, one of the signal tasks of a high school writing program is to help students develop their skill in the transactional modes: to write to inform or persuade; to work with subject matter that is outside of personal experience; to gather and organize raw materials, shaping them into discourse that accomplishes something with an audience. This means that teachers need to create purposes for writing that develop these abilities, but that are also meaningful and valuable and not just pretend writing or dummy runs. This in turn means writing tasks that offer genuine opportunities to explore, to investigate, to learn—and probably writing activities that retain a measure of student choice and decision making.

There are a number of writing activities that we would describe as being *transitional:* activities that build natural bridges between the narrative-expressive modes of writing appropriately stressed in the lower grades and the more challenging transactional modes increasingly required in high school and on into college. Such activities include reports from personal interviews or written surveys; descriptions of objects, persons, or places; analyses of social behavior, rituals, or values; comparisons of products used by students in their daily lives; and notes and letters related to personal or school issues. The keys to good transitional writing assignments are (1) making the work real and meaningful, (2) leaving plenty of authentic choices and decisions for the writer, and (3) engaging students in writing as a tool of learning, not as an exercise. Some helpful resources for developing such purposeful activities can be found in the following: *Learning to Write/Writing to Learn* (Mayher, Lester, and Pradl 1983), *Roots in the Sawdust* (Gere 1985), *Writing in the Content Areas* (Tchudi and Tchudi 1983), and *Language Connections* (Fulwiler and Young 1982).

4. *Experience in writing for a wide range of audiences, both inside and outside of school.*

Closely connected to the problem of purpose is the issue of audience. If students are to gain experience by writing for real purposes—to communicate, to think and learn, to create, and to express themselves—these purposeful writing experiences ought to be addressed to real and appropriate audiences. The alternative—directing all students' work to a single, unvaried teacher audience—undermines the integrity, reality, and trustworthiness of many valuable writing activities.

Unfortunately, steering all writing toward an unvaried teacher-reader is exactly what goes on in most school writing programs, for students of all linguistic backgrounds (Florio and Clark 1982a). In fact, as Britton (1975) points out, students' writing is not only funneled to a single audience, but this solitary audience—who is, after all, a human being of potentially rich and diverse ways of responding—

generally limits him- or herself to one particular role: the examiner. This traditional pattern bears much of the blame for the failure of writing instruction in American schools, because among other things it undermines the possibility of students making and communicating genuine meaning for a reader who might be interested in their messages. It replaces these crucial elements of real communication with tasks that result in what Florio calls "dead letters" (1979).

Writing for real audiences, on the other hand, has a number of positive benefits for student writers. To begin with, it provides the energy and motivation that comes from knowing that the work is real, not pretend (Judy 1980). The involvement of real audiences also gives students much-needed practice with one of a writer's most fundamental skills: adjusting discourse to the anticipated needs of the reader. If you always have the same reader, and that reader is always and only implicit, you are seriously handicapped in developing the conscious habits of thinking about, anticipating, and taking measures to meet the needs of specific real readers. When students are invited to write for a wide variety of audiences—even if some of them are imaginary—they learn to ask crucial authorial questions: What do my readers already know about this subject? What are their attitudes toward it? What terminology do they understand? What sort of tone will be most appropriate for them? How severely might spelling or grammatical errors interfere with the reception of my message? And so on.

Further, writing for varied, real audiences exerts a natural pressure to edit and revise the work. Students are willing to polish and refine their texts, not because a teacher demands it, but because they want their writing to achieve its purpose with a particular audience. And finally, writing for real audiences in many cases provides students with precious feedback: response about what in the writing was effective and about what did not work as well. Such response is likely to have a considerable effect upon a student's subsequent writing efforts—more so than heavy red-inked corrections from the teacher, an audience who as often as not knew the content of the writing before the writing ever began (Hays 1981, Beach 1979, Bamberg 1978).

Unfortunately, this kind of active practice with real audiences is very rare for students from nonmainstream groups, just as it generally is for other high school students. Some fortunate students may have out-of-school experiences that compensate for this lack; those who come from literacy-oriented backgrounds may have written letters and thank-you notes to distant relatives, had a pen-pal or distant correspondent, or used writing in play activities. Other students may not have had such experiences.

Nonmainstream students have a particular need for this sort of active practice with audiences for writing. Not only do they share the general need of all beginning writers to develop audience awareness and strategies for meeting various audiences' needs, but they face the additional challenge of needing to write for audiences whose oral language (and often some of their related language attitudes) differs somewhat from their own. In other words, nonmainstream students must write for mainstream teachers and others for whom the appearance of nonstandard-dialect features in a written text reduces the effectiveness of the message.

These student writers must come to terms not just with the rhetorical audience-adjusting that all writers do, but with the more diffuse expectation of many audiences that "good writing" employs standard English grammar and other mainstream patterns of language. Thus, for many mainstream students, learning to write essentially involves coming into the mature and sophisticated use of their own native dialect, whereas for nonmainstream students learning to write means mastering the sophisticated surface features, semantic structures, and discourse patterns of *another* dialect. However we describe the linguistic task these students face, it is a long reach, a great challenge. And teachers will not help students meet this challenge by simply declaiming the inventory of possible mistakes and the schedule of penalties audiences may exact. Students must learn to meet the demands of their audiences through the vigorous process of learning-in-use: practicing, experimenting, hypothesizing, getting responses, revising, and practicing some more.

In the classroom, audience becomes a positive focus of instruction when the teacher recognizes that most pieces of writing are in a sense incomplete and unreal until they eventually reach some kind of readership. It becomes a part of the teacher's job, then, just as important as creating assignments and responding to student drafts, to find ways in which students' written work can be addressed to real and distinct audiences. One excellent example is provided by the work of Heath and Branscombe (1985), who worked with a class of predominantly black ninth-grade students in doing extensive letter writing and community-based ethnographic research. The choice of letter writing was based on the assumption that "the development of written language depends upon a rich, responsive context" (p. 30) and that the students needed to learn that expository writing requires "linguistic devices and background information in explicated form if the addressee is to understand the writer" (p. 26). Over the course of a year, these students wrote long letters to people they did not know, receiving letters in return; as a result they accumulated extensive experience with written text, including a good deal of decontextualized expository prose. They used this experience as language input (as in oral language learning) "to *generate the needed internal rules or knowledge about how to make writing work* to communicate their feelings and knowledge" (p. 30). Thus students learned to use written language in ways similar to those of oral language acquisition—through "repeated trials and errors in attempting to communicate" (p. 31).

The Heath and Branscombe project suggests one set of activities and audiences; other researchers and practitioners have suggested many alternatives (Daniels and Zemelman 1985). The most evident and available alternative audience for student writing in almost any course is the roomful of other students, and many effective writing teachers have trained students to give various types of helpful responses to each others' work. In addition, the teacher can help students reach outside audiences, as well as diversifying his or her own roles of responding. Students may, in fact, write for a wide variety of audiences: for the teacher in roles other than examiner, for peer editing or response groups, for students in lower or higher grades, for students or teachers in other classes, for special in-school publications, for bulletins or newsletters sent outside of school, for hall displays, for school employees and officials, for students' own parents and families, for community agencies or officials, and for many other individuals and institutions farther removed from the school.

5. *Rich and continuous reading experience, including both published literature of acknowledged merit and the work of peers and instructors.*

Linguistic research on children's oral language development has shown that children unconsciously internalize and then experiment with patterns they hear in the speech going on around them. This phenomenon seems also to occur in the connection between reading and writing; that is, when children read, they unconsciously internalize the patterns of written language they are encountering at many levels, including vocabulary, sentence varieties, ways of addressing the reader, strategies for achieving textual cohesion, patterns of organization, means of supporting assertions or providing detail, and other elements of written language (Falk 1979).

Carl Bereiter and his colleagues (1980) have hypothesized that the ideas about writing that children thus acquire from their reading are organized as "genre schemes," or sets of patterns that constitute the basic requirements of (for example) fairy tales, recommendation letters, book reviews, and other genres of written language. If Bereiter is right, then his research describes one of the key differences between what skilled adult writers know and beginners don't—much of that knowledge deriving from the "passive" process of being immersed in models through reading. This understanding of the powerful role of reading experience in developing writing ability helps to explain why writing programs that stress reading as a part of the instructional process (Strom 1960, Emig 1982, Heys 1962, Blount 1973, Christensen 1967) have shown significant growth in students' performance. A somewhat more formalized variant of reading experience is the use of prose models as a teaching-learning strategy in writing instruction. Several studies have shown improved student writing performance after programs featuring such prose models (Hillocks 1986), and good descriptions of the related pedagogy are available (Eschholz 1980).

Students who use nonstandard dialects have a much higher incidence of reading difficulties than standard-English-speaking students, both in terms of their ability to decode and comprehend written texts and in their lack of broad out-of-school experience with the various genres of written language. In acknowledging this problem, it is important to remember that there is no evidence that the linguistic features of nonstandard dialects per se *cause* this lower achievement. Instead, the reasons for the differences in reading achievement seem to be primarily educational and cultural, and may involve not only cultural mismatches between children and schools but also the negative attitudes and low expectations of teachers already alluded to. In any case, the fact remains: these students come to the task of learning how to write with a somewhat weaker foundation in two areas—technical skill in reading, and knowledge of forms of written language gained from reading. Thus, if Bereiter is right—that children use internalized literary schemata in their writing—then this would seem to handicap students who read poorly and sparsely.

Without underestimating the seriousness of this special challenge for nonmainstream students, it is important to note that shortcomings in reading skill and experience plague all sorts of students. The stereotypical middle-class home full of the artifacts of literacy—books, newspapers, magazines, letters, lists on the refrigerator—may enhance, but does not guarantee, the acquisition of strong reading skills for

individual children. Nor does growing up in a nonmainstream house-
hold necessarily prevent a child from becoming a good reader and
writer. Just as with oral language, children need a relatively small
amount of raw material to learn from; they do not need to be heavily
bombarded with print input in order to start unraveling the puzzle of
literacy for themselves (Harste, Woodward, and Burke 1983). Moreover, not all middle-class homes abound with extensive opportunities
for literacy activities, and many nonmainstream homes do (Teale and
Sulzby, 1986).

There is another special reading problem shared by all students in
school: the lack of opportunity to read models or samples of the
specific sorts of writing that teachers may assign. Students are routinely asked to write book reports, dialogues, position papers, lab
reports, literary criticism, term papers, and other highly conventional-
ized genres of writing without ever having seen an example of such
discourse done well, either by a peer or a professional. Thus student
writers spend much time groping in the dark, trying to imagine or
invent the conventions of an assigned genre, when the opportunity to
absorb the characteristics of the form have been withheld. This practice is astonishingly counterproductive and extremely widespread, and
may create particular difficulties for nonmainstream students, who
generally have less exposure to expository modes of written language
(Heath and Branscombe 1985).

All of this clearly implies that teachers should foster reading
experiences as an integral part of writing instruction. Some class time
can be productively spent simply reading—silently or aloud—samples
of specific genres of writing that are about to be practiced in the
students' writing. For students not in the habit of reading at home, or
for whom the conditions for doing homework are not ideal, this kind
of class time is especially necessary. This reading should not be con-
fined to the work of published writers—as valuable as the experience
of good literature is. After all, students are not professional writers,
and offering them only and always such models risks that they will
never feel as successful as they may deserve to feel about their work.
Students should have ample opportunities to read and hear the work
of the other members of the class, including the teacher. A related
method for providing students with information about genres of writing is the use of scales related to particular assignments. In this
approach, the teacher not only provides model papers but also a
rubric or protocol that specifies the criteria for an effective response to
the assignment. Students working with such scales—for example,

using them in revising their own work—have shown significant gains in several studies (Sager 1973; Coleman 1982; Clifford 1978, 1981).

6. *Exposure to models of writing in process and writers at work, including both teachers and classmates.*

If a student's reading experience helps him or her become familiar with the *products* of writing, he or she also needs to learn about the *process* by which these final products are gradually created by real adult and student writers. Yet, one of the ironic inefficiencies of traditional school writing instruction is that the learners rarely get a chance to see skilled practitioners (e.g., teachers, older students) actually working at the craft. Though there has been little empirical research that separates this factor from other elements of instruction, a number of leading composition theorists (Moffet 1968, Perl 1983) and program developers (Graves 1983) have pointed out this strange omission of modeling from writing instruction. They remind us that classroom teachers who routinely demonstrate their own skills in speaking, listening, and reading hardly ever write in front of, or along with, their students.

Some mainstream students can draw upon family or other out-of-school experience with older writers; indeed, their parents may work every day with pens, typewriters, word processors, reports, briefs, periodicals, or books. For many other students, however, the lack of firsthand modeling leaves them in the dark as to how "real" writers work. After all, many nonmainstream students come from homes where writing is not a central part of their parents' occupations or of family affairs, and where the rates of parental illiteracy are high.

If students have little experience with seeing writers at work, they are likely to develop misconceptions of what skilled writers actually do. For example, one of the most common and destructive myths among students of all linguistic backgrounds is that the better a writer you become, the more orderly, swift, and painless your writing process will be. This delusion can become a terrible handicap if one's own writing process feels labored and seems, in the absence of any model to the contrary, to be a wrong way of working.

School programs that feature teachers writing along with students have reported overall success, although the modeling variable has not been measured separately. Probably the best known program stressing the importance of modeling is that of Donald Graves (1983), which has been adopted by schools around the country and has had a great impact upon the training provided by the National Writing Project.

In Graves's approach, the classroom becomes a writing workshop or studio where everyone, including the teacher, is engaged in the craft of writing. The teacher also has a special responsibility to demonstrate his or her own writing process, display drafts from various stages of his or her own writing in progress, and share his or her writing when students read pieces aloud. In other words, the teacher joins in the activity of the studio as a master of the craft, modeling skilled performance along with giving instruction and technical assistance.

Why does this modeling seem to be so valuable? Students, especially those for whom writing is a rare event outside of school, may need to watch adult writers actually working: starting, stopping, getting stuck, doodling, grumbling, crumpling up papers and throwing away false starts, establishing a flow, resting, getting frustrated, crossing out and adding elements, rereading chunks, and staring into space. It is usually not the imagined neat and effortless process, but a rather messy, ad hoc, and very personal struggle against white empty space. Similarly, students can benefit to a degree from studying facsimiles of the revised drafts of published writing or the work of an adult model in school.

Who provides all this modeling in the classroom? Obviously, the teacher is the most available adult candidate. First, the teacher can demonstrate his or her own composing processes as Graves recommends, using an overhead projector or flip-chart pad, verbalizing the thinking involved in selecting a topic, planning an approach, generating a draft, and making revisions and corrections. The teacher can then post some of his or her own rough drafts in the classroom, showing the path of the revision strategies. Other adults in the school can be solicited to either demonstrate or talk about their own writing processes, implicitly reminding students that accomplished adult writers have a variety of ways of working. Of course, fellow students are another important source of modeling, although they are more likely to have a mixture of effective and ineffective working strategies. Perhaps even more productively, students can be encouraged to talk over the problems they encounter during the processes of writing and revising, sharing ideas for getting over the difficult moments. For students from nonmainstream groups it will also be powerful for them to hear from skilled writers from their own cultural group— people who can demonstrate, either explicitly or implicitly, ways in which a nonmainstream speaker-writer can learn to make the necessary adjustments and accommodations in real writing tasks.

By way of summary: all the activities under the heading of modeling are aimed at helping students get around a peculiar school-bred impediment to their mastery of writing. Teachers are always commanding students to write, and then using the products of these commands as the main input for the school reward system—and yet students almost never have a chance to observe, reflect on, and discuss how this work gets done by people who are good at it.

7. *Instruction in the processes of writing; that is, learning to work at a given writing task in appropriate phases, including prewriting, drafting, and revising.*

One of the key insights from the past decade of research on writing has been the "process" view of writing, the realization that composing is not a single act but a sequence of differentiated and recursive activities (Flower and Hayes 1981a, Murray 1968). While the term *writing process* has become sufficiently popularized that it now adorns the covers of commercial textbooks, the insight it stands for remains valuable. Student writers who have learned to approach writing as a series of steps or stages have performed well in experimental studies. In Hillocks's (1986) meta-analysis of four modes of writing instruction, the two modes that stress a process approach to instruction ("environmental" and "natural process") showed the highest levels of overall writing growth.

Though there are any number of competing models of the writing process circulating in the literature, most of them offer, more or less, a division into a triumvirate of stages: prewriting, drafting, and revising. Sometimes under differing terminology researchers have isolated the individual stages of the process for study. Prewriting, broadly defined as structured activities designed to help students gather and organize material for writing, has been associated with improved performance in a number of studies (Rohman and Wlecke 1964, Young and Koen 1973, Burns 1980, Odell 1974, Emig 1971, Cooper 1973, Stallard 1974). Similarly, students who have learned strategies for revision—ways of reseeing and rewriting their original drafts—tend to produce better essays than writers without such revising skills (Hansen 1978, Sommers 1979, Bamberg 1978, Faigley and Witte 1981).

Perhaps the reason the process approach to writing has been so effective with students and so popular with teachers is that it dispels one of the key fears inexperienced writers suffer: the need to get everything right the first time (Elbow 1973). Once the understanding takes hold that one can generate an imperfect rough draft, not worrying about gaps and errors, and then come back later to mend, expand, and revise, it can be a revelation. Too many students are frozen by their own contrary conception, that writing is not a series of activities that gradually results in a product but rather a one-chance-only performance that mostly seems to offer a brief, conspicuous opportunity to fail.

The process approach model of writing instruction is now filtering slowly into public school practice, most quickly into the wealthy, culturally mainstream schools able to afford the kind of intensive teacher retraining needed to support such a profound shift in instruction. However, inservice training is not the only factor involved. Many schools enrolling a high proportion of nonmainstream students lag behind in the implementation of a process approach because they have capitulated to what education officials see as the students' chaotic out-of-school lives and lack of orientation toward the future. In such schools, each day and each lesson tend to become compartmentalized and discontinuous; rarely are projects initiated that span a number of phases over a length of time. And yet, ironically, it is clear that working persistently at a task over time, developing a product through a patient and purposeful series of steps, is a skill without which real academic success is unlikely.

The ability of nonmainstream students to approach writing as a series of differentiated steps may also have been compromised by previous instruction. If past teachers have scrupulously marked every error (both dialect-based and other types) on every paper that a student has ever written, this may have confirmed for the student that the writing process is something he or she will never master. Instead, the student needs to learn that eliminating all these errors is part of the work of the revising stage in the writing process and that he or she can develop a strategy of writing a first draft in fluent, comfortable, personal language, just to get the shape of the ideas down, and then return later—in a separate and unhurried step—to reshape the draft into something even more meaningful and also more correct.

Teaching writing as a process, as a series of steps a writer takes to develop and refine a text, offers an excellent opportunity—especially for these nonmainstream students—not just to write better but to practice the crucial academic skill of refining a piece of work over time. The teacher's main job is to break writing projects into stages and institutionalize these stages in the classroom. This means devising prewriting activities that provide both time and methods for gathering and organizing material. It means providing drafting time in class, with feedback and technical assistance available from the teacher and peers. It means treating revision as a normal and essential part of the work of writing, with time, resources, and collaborative effort being devoted to helping authors rewrite. Individual pieces may go through several drafts over time, in between which they rest in the student's folder while ideas percolate and the author's distance from the original text healthily increases. There is perhaps no moment more emblematic of both intellectual development and delayed gratification than when a student removes a months-old draft from his or her writing folder and sets to work, with new vigor and insight, on yet another draft.

8. *Collaborative activities for students that provide ideas for writing and guidance for revising works in progress.*

Some of the more widely adopted "new" practices in the teaching of writing are classroom activities in which students assist each other in various stages of writing (Bruffee 1980, Elbow 1973). In Hillocks's (1986) meta-analysis of experimental studies, such student collaboration (in both the "environmental" and the "natural process" modes of instruction) was associated with greater gains in writing quality than the noncollaborative "presentational" and "individualized" approaches.

This harnessing of collaborative spirit is manifested in school programs in two main ways. The writing workshop approach (Graves 1983, Calkins 1983, Haas et al. 1972), which has been especially favored in elementary schools, provides unstructured, continuous, and free-flowing student collaboration on pieces of writing and on specific writing problems. At the secondary level peer editing or response groups are the more common collaborative practice. In this procedure, groups of three to five students serve as each other's regular audience, editors, or collaborators. The literature shows a great variety in the ways that such groups may be selected, how they are trained, how much teacher guidance they receive, how long they remain together, and so forth. Still, a wide variety of peer-group structures for writing classes have been successful in improving students' writing performance (Clifford 1981, Braddock 1963, Diederich 1974, Beaven 1977, Elbow 1973, Dow 1973, Lagana 1972, Perl 1985).

It is possible that such peer collaboration may build in an especially constructive way upon the cultural resources that many nonmainstream students bring to school. As Mina Shaughnessy has said in describing her classroom work with minority students, "Precisely because writing is a social act, a kind of synthesis that is reached through the dialectic of discussion, the teaching of writing must often begin with the experience of dialogue and end with the experience of a real audience, not only of teachers but of peers" (1977, p. 83).

As we mentioned in Chapter 2, some (though not all) nonmainstream communities have been shown to use writing in a more social and interactive way than the more solitary and individualistic ways of mainstream culture. Of course, all groups include many verbal styles in their repertoires. However, most nonmainstream cultures do not use the mainstream patterns of speech on which school literacy is based. The school, typically operating as a symbol and agent of middle-class styles of behaving, has an opportunity both to respect and actually make use of a unique cultural strength that many nonmainstream students bring with them to school.

Still, implementing peer collaboration isn't necessarily easier among nonmainstream students than among others. To begin with, if children have been treated as stupid and incompetent throughout their formal schooling (as many of these students may have been), the victims of such low expectations may internalize this disrespect both for themselves and for their classmates: the result is that students come to believe that neither they nor their peers could have anything valuable to offer a teacher, or each other. Closely related to this is the problem that most of these adolescents have already spent at least eight previous years in institutions that try to socialize all communal and cooperative instincts out of children in order to instill the mainstream value system of competitive individualism. And there may also be numerous special, local problems—the tone of the school, conflicts among peer subgroups, the intrusion of outside distractions—that work against peer collaboration, especially with schools in tumultuous school districts or economically disadvantaged neighborhoods.

Therefore, teachers who elect to use some form of peer collaboration in the classroom can't simply implement it; students must be prepared to work constructively and purposefully together beforehand. The chances are that this preparation will take some time and care, whatever the cultural style of the community the school serves. Students need to be shown that they can, for example, take their own and others' work seriously, make a valuable response to a peer's work, criticize without injuring, divide up the available time in a small group and make sure everyone gets the help they need, and so forth. But all of these understandings need to be assured by purposeful training before collaborative activities begin to focus on the real written work of class members. Therefore, a helpful step in preparation is for students to study examples of real student writing—both strong and weak—from unidentified students in other places. Working with such samples, peers can practice responding carefully and pointedly to real student work, but wait to critique each other's work until they have developed the necessary habits of seriousness, insight, and tact.

9. One-to-one writing conferences with the teacher.

While there has long been agreement among practicing teachers that individual conferences provide an ideal structure for careful development of beginning writers, the demands of the public school setting have made this instructional approach seem a luxurious and logistically unworkable dream. Teachers have agreed enthusiastically with theorists like Donald Murray (1968), who validate their faith in conferences, but they typically assume that only college professors with low student loads can actually implement this strategy.

Recently, though, a number of researchers and practitioners, led by Donald Graves, have been actively developing and testing programs that provide for frequent one-to-one writing conferences between teachers and student authors. Graves has implemented this practice extensively in elementary school classrooms with significant results. In his 1982 report on a three-year study of the development of student writers, he identified conferences as the single most important instructional strategy in the program, the one most responsible for growth in student writing performance. And in his subsequent book, *Writing: Teachers and Children at Work* (1983), Graves explained in detail the procedures he developed for conducting various kinds of student conferences. Susan Sowers, one of Graves's research associates, conducted an ethnographic study (1979) of the conferences that occurred in one of Graves's experimental classrooms and documented the growth in the work of young student writers. Lucy Calkins, another associate of Graves, conducted a case study focused in part upon the impact of both formal and informal conferences on one girl's growth as an author (1983).

Why does the conference method seem to be so effective? It seems likely that teacher-student conferences provide what Jerome Bruner (1978) has called "scaffolding," a mechanism by which a more experienced learner or thinker provides intellectual scaffolds—temporary support structures—that assist a learner in developing new ways of thinking.

Certainly students from nonmainstream groups would benefit from one-to-one teacher conferences at least as much as other students. But at present, these student writers probably enjoy fewer conferences than mainstream students for a number of reasons. As we have said, the urban schools that many of these students attend tend to emphasize a skill-drill approach to learning and accordingly favor teacher-centered, whole-class instruction. The conference method requires teachers who are willing and able to work with students one-on-one, and also requires that schools provide teachers the retraining and inservice support necessary to nurture this innovation; sadly, both of these elements are too often lacking in many of the schools that nonmainstream students attend. Possibly even more important, these schools typically have large class sizes, which makes it difficult for teachers to orchestrate individual conferences with student writers. This reveals the one shortcoming of the conference as a teaching technique: it is highly sensitive to class size. A teacher can conduct significantly longer and more frequent conferences with a class of twenty students than with a class of thirty-five.

Concerns about classroom discipline can also work against the implementation of writing conferences. In schools where control of students is viewed as a major problem, either because of (ironically) unmanageably large class sizes or because students come from a culture that seems alien to the school, teachers may become preoccupied with control and fearful of trying anything new—especially a method that doesn't offer direct face-to-face teacher control over the whole group. After all, for conferences to work, the teacher must first establish work assignments for everyone in the class, activities that continue while the teacher turns his or her attention to a series of individual students. Usually, what goes on during this time is a writing workshop, in which students can work at planning, drafting, and revising their writing; exchanging drafts quietly with each other; reading peers' work and writing critiques; and the like. If the teacher cannot get the rest of the class to work in this kind of sustained, orderly, independent way, conferences become impossible.

Whatever the hurdles, conferences are worth the effort, and perhaps especially so for students from nonmainstream cultures. For adolescents who feel alien to the school culture, whose experiences with literacy instruction have left them feeling like failures, and who may be catastrophically lacking in sheer experience with the written word, someone needs to take a personal interest in their individual development. Ideally, a caring and literate adult needs to show each student directly and personally that writing can become an avenue of accomplishment—that regardless of his or her past experience, the student can now begin to use language in school in a new way, starting by making meaning of his or her own experiences and sharing these with a concerned, trustworthy audience, and gradually growing outward from that point. These students need to have the experience of having an adult audience take their written work seriously, "receiving" the writing (as Graves calls it), sitting with them side-by-side at a table contemplating the next move in the process of developing a piece of work.

10. Direct instruction in specific strategies and techniques for writing.
Much recent composition research has helped us to recognize the natural, active language-learning capacities of students; we have been reminded that students can learn by practicing writing, sharing their work with others, hearing the responses of peer readers, and so forth. But in recognizing the value of these "naturalistic" processes, we must not forget that there are also important roles for the teacher beyond being an audience, a model, and an organizer of peer groups. In the teacher's repertoire, there is a place for active instruction, too. Recent research suggests, however, that writing teachers may need to learn some active instructional roles different from the ones they have habitually played.

Many aspects of the standard method of teaching writing have proved to be truly ineffective. In Hillocks's (1986) meta-analysis, the traditional "presentational" mode was described as including lectures and teacher-led discussions of specific rules or concepts related to writing, followed by writing exercises in which students practiced the chosen rules or concepts with feedback from the teacher. This method of instruction was the *least* effective by a wide margin when compared with the three other main approaches to teaching writing (environmental, natural process, and individualized).

Even on the fundamental teacher practice of assignment making, the research raises questions. As Graves (1983) and Florio and Clark (1982a) have pointed out, the traditional practice of having students write to teacher-designed writing assignments can be counterproductive. When an instructor takes responsibility for specifying the topic, purpose, and audience, as well as dictating all the procedures for working, the student writer's autonomy and responsibility are stripped away. Students who get such "assignments" aren't really being asked to do what writers do (that is, develop a whole piece of meaningful discourse by means of a series of actions and decisions with language); rather, they are filling in the blanks in someone else's predetermined discourse. Graves and others have spoken eloquently about the need for teachers to let individual student writers make the hard choices, to develop their own voice, their own sense of authorship, their own feelings of responsible ownership of their written work.

On the other hand, Hillocks's (1986) study and others (Freedman et al. 1985) point the way to a different set of methods that writing teachers should use. In Hillocks's view, the most effective mode of instruction is the "environmental," in which the teacher (1) selects "clear and specific objectives," (2) provides "materials and problems selected to engage students with each other in specifiable processes important to some specific aspect of writing," and (3) arranges "activities . . . conducive to high levels of peer interaction" (p. 122). As Hillocks describes it, this kind of teaching places "teacher and student more nearly in balance, with the teacher planning activities and selecting materials through which students interact with each other to generate ideas and learn identifiable writing skills" (p. 123).

Elsewhere in his analysis, Hillocks offers further examples of direct and active teaching behavior, some of which are centered around providing students with sets of data and tools for analyzing them. He also points to studies by Scardamalia, Bereiter, and Goelman (1982) and Anderson, Bereiter, and Smart (1980) that argue (Graves's studies notwithstanding) for a more active role for teachers in assignment making. Students in these studies who were given teacher-made assignments, combined with effective prewriting activities or with "contentless encouragement" during drafting, produced up to twice as much writing as students who had complete autonomy over their topics. One way of summarizing this strand of research is to note that it calls for a variety of highly active, participatory, experiential roles for *both* teachers and students, in contrast to the traditional writing classroom where the teacher is the active one and students sit passively, receiving instructions, advice, exhortations, and warnings.

The need for this sort of teaching and learning observes no dialect boundaries. It is fundamentally important that students learn to see writing as a valuable tool for learning and for solving real problems, and these kinds of guided activities reinforce that basic outlook. In schools that enroll a high proportion of nonmainstream students, direct instruction can also focus on the special issues that nonmainstream writers face. As long as care is taken not to enshrine dialect variations as the core of the writing curriculum, valuable exercises can be devised that help students grapple with the mismatch between their oral language and the dialect expected in much school writing. For example, a teacher can provide activities to help students "translate" from their vernacular into a more formal register, thus developing a skill that is helpful in the revising stage of the writing process. Student writers might also benefit from role-playing some of the audiences they need to be able to communicate with—people with different linguistic backgrounds and accompanying language attitudes—in order to reinforce the need to anticipate the reactions of such readers to particular dialect features or deviations from standard written language.

11. Reduced instruction in grammatical terminology and related drills, with increased use of sentence combining activities.

One of the most thoroughly researched questions in language arts education is the relationship between the teaching of formal grammar and the improvement of writing ability. The term *formal grammar* as used here refers mainly to grammatical terminology (names of parts of speech) and sentence diagramming or parsing, activities that still consume a good deal of time in many elementary and secondary schools. Scores of research studies have been conducted on this topic since the turn of the century, and the vast majority have shown no positive correlation between grammar training and writing quality (Hatfield 1935, Strom 1960, Braddock 1963, Elley et al. 1976, Hillocks 1986). In fact, a number of studies have shown a negative relationship between instruction in formal grammar and writing performance, though the deterioration probably does not result from specific harm done by grammatical instruction but rather by time being stolen away from the practice of actual writing (Petrosky 1977, Hillocks 1986).

If any educational case ought to have been closed by the verdict from research, it is the one of formal grammar and writing. And yet, in spite of vast documentation, most working teachers do not accept these findings and continue to conduct formal grammar lessons, as in most districts the school curriculum requires. Obviously, grammar is deeply and very specially rooted in the structure of American schooling, and no amount of empirical evidence seems capable of dislodging it from its central role in the curriculum. (Several recent historical studies by Daniels [1983], Baron [1982], and Heath [1980] have explored the relationships between the American teaching profession and conceptions of grammar, linguistic propriety, and standard English.)

For our own part, we certainly do not oppose the teaching of formal grammar as a school subject. As a matter of fact, we happen to believe that the study of language is at the heart of the humanities. The understanding of human language is so supremely important that we think every American schoolchild should have many more opportunities to explore the descriptive study of language; to learn about the history and development of languages, language families, and dialects; to study the universals as well as the contrasts among different tongues; to analyze how languages operate, using rule-governed systems of phonology, syntax, semantics, pragmatics, and discourse; to examine how languages change over time; to become aware of the complex social diemensions of language use; to learn about the relationships between language and thought; to find out how children acquire their native oral language and apply the insights of that process to other kinds of learning. Nevertheless, though we appreciate the importance of all these studies, we recognize that having abstract descriptive knowledge about linguistic phenomena does not necessarily help a person *use* language in any particular way, any more than knowing the names of the concentric organs of a tree (xylem, phloem, cambrium, etc.) will help you grow one, climb one, or cut one down. So we think it is with formal, conscious grammatical knowledge and learning to write.

A much better reason for teaching grammar, we believe, is that through grammar teachers and students can enjoy a common meta-language with which to talk about sentences in written texts. While we know that some writing teachers (including one of us) can comfortably discuss sentences with students without such a *lingua franca*, many teachers find it a useful tool. The question becomes one of time. If it takes scores of hours, grade after grade, year after year throughout schooling to teach this metalanguage, and if students by and large do not successfully learn it so that they are able to use it, what is the point of all this instructional time? If we also believe that practice is a key element of learning to write, then we have to balance the expenditure of time on grammatical knowledge with students' need to gain writing practice in school.

Why doesn't grammar instruction work the way teachers wish it did? Probably the main reason is that it consists of teaching *about* writing instead of teaching writing. In other words, it offers students a high-level abstraction—a metalanguage—that they apparently find hard to draw upon in their actual school work. Another approach to working with grammatical structure—sentence combining—has been considerably more successful. Pioneered by John Mellon (1969), Kellogg Hunt (1970), Frances Christensen (1967), Frank O'Hare (1973), and Morenberg (1980), this strategy gives students practice in combining short "kernel" sentences into longer, more complex (or "syntactically mature") sentences, using the wide variety of sentence expansion techniques available in English. Instead of teaching students *about* sentence patterns, this approach helps students actually generate the alternative patterns through structured practice, not precept. Students expand their repertoire of sentence types experientially, drawing upon their internal sense of grammaticality (their linguistic competence) to accept or reject possible patterns as they practice. A noteworthy outcome of sentence combining activity is that while it focuses only on the development of sentence patterns, it seems to raise the general quality ratings given by expert readers in experimental studies (Mellon 1969, Cooper 1975, Stotsky 1975, Combs 1976).

If we know that the study of formal grammar does not enhance student writing performance, then there is no reason to spend much time on such activities in writing programs for students of any linguistic backgound. Unfortunately, there is a tendency among school officials to believe that students who speak nonstandard dialects are *especially* in need of such instruction. Perhaps this insistence on teaching formal grammar to nonmainstream students is really more a part of what Goodlad (1984) and others have called the "hidden curriculum," the implicit set of lessons schools teach about the approved values of the mainstream culture. In any case, even though there are no separate studies of its effect on nonstandard-dialect speakers as compared with others, it seems likely that sentence combining should be an effective alternative for nonmainstream students as well. After all, the operating principle of sentence combining is active exploration and meaningful practice with sentences, rather than the more abstract, analytical activities of traditional formal grammar instruction. Teachers seeking to utilize sentence combining activities in the classroom may choose from a wide variety of commercial materials, or they can quite easily design their own exercises keyed to the specific needs and interests of their students.

Even if we discard "formal grammar" from the writing curriculum, replacing it with the syntactic practice of sentence combining, it is evident that there are still many grammatical features that nonmainsteam students need to learn to recognize, understand, and consciously control. They need to know which features of their own oral dialect are highly stigmatized, and they should add the contrasting standard form to their writing repertoire, for use when they need it. Yet, as we said earlier, this does not mean making error the center of the curriculum, or teaching a great number of standard English rules "before students can write." Instead, it is essentially a matter of helping students become skillful at reseeing and revising drafts of their own writing.

As students learn how to revise, and as they practice preparing their work for various audiences, it becomes appropriate and productive for the teacher to address specific dialect-based grammar issues as they arise in the actual work—verb tense markings, subject-verb agreement, usage contrasts, and the like—offering and explaining the contrasting standard forms where useful. Of course, for a writing instructor to be able to do this requires that he or she know what linguistic features of the student's particular nonstandard dialect contrast sharply with the written standard. The fundamental linguistic principles outlined in Chapter 2 of this book can be a starting point, but the teacher must also develop a careful and sensitive attention to the actual language use of each student. In the next section, we deal further with the question of error.

12. *Teaching of writing mechanics and grammar in the context of students' actual compositions, rather than in separate drills or exercises.*

One way of understanding the general failure of American writing instruction is to notice that the schools have typically taught the last things first. There is no better example of this than the enormous amount of teacher time devoted to warning students about the various errors of writing mechanics—by which we mean spelling, punctuation, usage, and manuscript conventions—that they might make, when and if they ever wrote. Ironically, these mechanical skills are the elements of writing consistently proven to need *the least* attention in the National Assessment's studies of American students' writing over the past seventeen years. The critical problems identified by NAEP have been with much higher-order (and generally undertaught) skills, such as intersentence coherence, supporting details for main points, organization of information, and the like. Still, in many classrooms, much time is spent on drill-and-practice exercises in which writing mechanics are decontextualized, disembedded from the kinds of meaningful contexts in which they might be mastered relatively naturally. A corollary problem, about which teachers often complain, is that while students do develop mastery in drill situations, when they write real texts, the errors "mastered" in drills promptly reappear. This phenomenon reminds us that writing, like other aspects of language use, is probably acquired holistically, that is, in use (Falk 1979) rather than as a cumulative sequence of subskills (Birnbaum 1981).

In Hillocks's (1986) meta-analysis of alternative focuses of writing instruction, the category that included the kind of decontextualized lessons described above proved to be the only negative approach studied, resulting in an average loss in writing quality among students in five experimental studies. The main alternative is to address mechanics in the context of students' real writing, viewing this work essentially as a part of revising or editing. Obviously this approach has roots in the writing process research cited earlier. Graves's study in New Hampshire schools (1982) was a key validation of this approach; though mechanical skills were taught only as the need to use them arose in student writing, and were usually taught either in individual conferences or in brief small-group lessons, the students in this program showed the expected grade-level growth in the mastery of mechanics over the year. These students also made exceptional gains in writing performance. Other researchers have confirmed the value of teaching mechanics in the context of real writing (Adams 1971; Calkins 1979, 1980; King and Rentel 1983; Hailey 1978).

Much as with the issue of teaching formal grammar, students who speak nonstandard dialects are often viewed as needing even more intensive instruction in writing mechanics than other students. Perhaps because they may be more inexperienced with writing and with reading standard expository text, they may indeed show less mastery of these elements, but this doesn't make decontextualized drills any more valuable. As we've already asserted, the best solution is to help students develop skill, experience, resources, and good working habits in revising their own writing.

None of this means that nonmainstream students do not need to work actively at the problems of error in their writing—prominently including, but not limited to, errors that occur because of the influence of nonstandard oral dialects. As the principles already reviewed suggest, however, attention to these errors by teachers and students must occur in a program of writing instruction that includes some key elements: positive attitudes and expectations on the teacher's part, a great deal of writing practice, and awareness of the stages in the process of writing, as well as the provision of meaningful response to work in progress, a feeling of personal authority and choice for student authors, regular opportunities for teacher conferences and peer collaboration, and so forth. In such an environment, it becomes possible and appropriate for the teacher to teach the mechanics of writing. After all, in this kind of writing program, he or she will be offering helpful tricks of the trade to an audience of writers who have immediate use for the tricks.

As we have already noted, Mina Shaughnessy's *Errors and Expectations* (1977) offers detailed and useful guidance for teachers dealing with error in the work of nonmainstream adolescents. Though her book reports on work with "basic" writers in a college open-enrollment program, the kinds of students and writing errors are very similar to those we are discussing here. Shaughnessy takes errors very seriously, and a main goal in her classroom is for students to eliminate surface errors from their writing. Attention to these errors is important, Shaughnessy argues, not so much for their own sake but because these students, throughout their years of difficulty with school writing tasks, have come to associate their own mechanical and grammatical errors with the pain and failure of writing. She believes that, in order to establish some sense of competence and control over written language, these students must conquer some of their persistent errors. Even so, Shaughnessy recommends spending no more than 20 percent of class time talking about errors and teaching the correct forms. The rest of the time should be devoted to higher-level rhetorical issues and to the practicing and sharing of written work.

13. Moderate marking of surface structure errors, focusing on sets or patterns of related errors.

Many teachers believe that the most fundamental and conspicuous obligation of a writing instructor is to mark every error in every paper that every student ever writes. This tradition is also strongly perpetuated by parents: because their children's writing is essentially the only tangible evidence they ever receive of what goes on in school, and because it was the way they themselves were taught, parents tend to attach great significance to the thoroughness with which the teacher roots out and red-pencils each mistake in their children's papers.

All this conscientious and laborious attention to student work, however, is not positively related to improvement in student writing quality. In fact, a number of studies have shown no difference in the subsequent writing performance of students—whether the marking of their papers was intensive or moderate, or whether the comments stressed praise or criticism (Dieterich 1972, Cooper 1974, Beach 1979, Arnold 1963, Bamberg 1978). An important rejoinder to these findings is offered by Hillocks, who showed in a 1982 study that teacher marking of papers can be considerably more powerful than this other research suggests if it is done in the context of a very intensive, process-oriented program of writing instruction.

There is a sense in which these findings should not surprise us. Students—even high school students—are beginners at writing, and as such they will inevitably make many mistakes. So it is with all language-learning activities—acquiring one's native oral language, learning to read—as well as most other activities human beings learn. For an audience to fixate upon errors of form is to engage in a kind of feedback that is not useful to learners in other linguistic contexts and doesn't seem to be with writing either. When children are learning to speak or read, many parents and teachers instinctively respond to, praise, and build on the things that the child can do well. One of the key traits of a skillful helper, in fact, is the ability to overlook almost all errors and to discern and respond to the meaning that the child is trying to make, regardless of how approximate it may be. Unfortunately, we have traditionally taken the opposite approach in writing instruction: being obsessed from the very start with all the things children can do wrong, teaching them about errors, circling their errors, counting up their errors. If oral language or reading were taught from the same error-oriented view, we would probably be living in a speechless, illiterate world.

The ineffectiveness of heavy correction apparently stems from students' inability to make use of such feedback as a paper covered with red marks and marginal comments. Teachers who mark papers intensively report frequent experiences with students who, upon having a paper returned with such feedback, promptly crumple it up and throw it into the wastebasket—discarding in the process a good deal of the teacher's own time. It may be that students, feeling personal investment in their written work, take heavily corrected papers as a personal attack. Or it may be that the complexity and quantity of such a response is simply overwhelming.

Whenever this approach to responding to student writing is given a justification, which is rarely, the rationale is usually that it prevents errors from "taking root." Clearly the strategy is a failure, and errors "take root" anyway, as most high school teachers will testify. Further, this approach to error marking creates another problem, a phenomenon that teachers call the "paper load." Because marking every error in every student paper takes so much of their own out-of-school time, teachers only assign as much writing practice as they can mark, and that amount is usually not enough for students to become practiced writers. Indeed, this somewhat ironic bottleneck—after all, it is caused by teachers with "high standards"—is one of the main reasons that American students haven't practiced writing enough to get good at it. And finally, students whose writing includes features from stigmatized nonstandard dialects are, once again, more likely than others to receive such scrupulous red-penciling, since they are thought to "need it" even more desperately than the rest.

As the research on paper marking has suggested, students seem unable to isolate and learn from patterns of error when their papers are covered with red. It seems much more effective for teachers to identify one or two sets of related errors that may or may not be dialect-related, helping students to focus their attention on a manageable set of problems as they draft their next piece of writing. If the student does not understand the error the teacher has identified, then it can be taught, either in individual conference or to a group of students who share the same problem. There is even some question about whether a teacher should actually mark each instance of an error pattern. After all, if students don't eventually learn to locate and repair their own errors, they haven't assumed full responsibility as writers. In response to this problem, some teachers offer students an oral or written comment that guides them toward needed corrections without flagging each instance.

Errors are not just evidence of ignorance for teachers to circle and students to correct. The mistakes that any student makes in his or her writing offer teachers rich and detailed evidence of what the student *does* know. As Shaughnessy asserts, beneath the superficial "chaos of error" that may infest some student papers, "a closer look will reveal very little that is random or 'illogical'" in the writing of nonmainstream students (1977, p. 5). Errors tell a great deal about students' knowledge of the conventions of written language, the cognitive strategies they use in writing, the contrasts between their home language and the official language of school, the level of attention they are able to muster in revision, and other matters (Shaughnessy 1977, Bartholomae 1984).

For example, if a student omits half of the required past-tense markers in a piece of writing, a teacher may assume that he or she "just doesn't understand" past tenses. Yet a close study of the actual error pattern may reveal something else; if the student produces irregular past-tense forms correctly, this, along with the scattering of correctly marked regular forms, suggests that he or she does indeed "understand" the idea of past tense. Instead, the problem is that certain phonological features of the student's oral language "encourage" the consonant cluster reductions that are transcribed in the writing, and the student is later catching only a handful of them in the revision stage. Analyzing error in this way gives a teacher vital information that can guide instruction. In this case, the student doesn't need an explanation of the taught past tense; what is needed is for the student to understand the contrast in this particular feature between speaking and writing, and to practice editing for a form the student already is using in some contexts. There are many other similar examples, but the basic point should be clear: teachers have much to learn from the close and nonjudgmental study of the writing that students actually produce.

Contemporary technology may offer writing teachers another approach to dealing with errors in writing. Certain of the newer microcomputer word-processing programs, like Writer's Workbench, can be programmed to flag certain kinds of dialect-based grammatical errors (e.g., missing tense markers). The time spent with such an editing program can be entirely individualized, using pieces of the student's own writing—a tremendous advantage over the more common drill programs—and can offer students a chance to work privately on recurrent errors in their writing without requiring teacher or whole-class time devoted to these matter.

14. Flexible and cumulative evaluation of student writing that stresses revision and is sensitive to variations in subject, audience, and purpose.

Too often in school writing programs, pieces of writing are killed off by premature evaluation. Instead of using evaluation as a formative process, steering students into and through a series of revisions, teachers often feel pressure to evaluate summatively, awarding a grade to a first or single draft, which often stunts the prospects for revision. Indeed, once a piece has been officially judged and labeled, it is hard for a student (or any other writer) to gather the energy for another draft.

The formative-summative dichotomy is directly to the point. The writing process research cited above strongly recommends that teachers should implement revision in the classroom. Instruction shouldn't focus on catching and punishing the weaknesses of early drafts, but rather on helping students develop additional stronger drafts. In practice, this doesn't mean that teachers should not read and respond to student work; there is every indication that some early reader response can be of critical help to writers (Diederich 1974, Dieterich 1972, Braddock 1963, Cooper 1974) as long as it takes a constructive form. The overall finding from recent research suggests that the most helpful response does not consist of indiscriminate praise nor of unrelieved criticism, but a balance of the two, with praise predominating (Van-DeWeghe 1978, Dieterich 1972, Cooper 1974).

Once the formative kinds of evaluation have been used to steer students through a full writing process with a given piece, the exigencies of schooling may require that a grade be assigned. Deciding how to handle summative evaluation requires that teachers consider many aspects of the research already reviewed. To begin with, it is clear that in an exemplary, research-based writing program, there can be no single "correct" way of grading or rating student work. If writing is done for a variety of real audiences, for different real purposes, in a variety of forms, and with any number of other variations and uniquenesses, then thoughtful teachers will develop a wide repertoire of evaluation strategies. At one extreme, teachers may well decide not to put grades of any kind on students' personal autobiographical writing, feeling that such an action violates the real purpose and value of such writing. On the other hand, teachers may develop quite complex analytic scales for assessing the content and form of formal academic research papers (Hillocks 1986).

Let us consider once more the relative weight traditionally assigned to form and content, especially as it relates to the special problems of nonmainstream student writers. What about those papers filled with nonstandard-dialect features? Are we going to reinforce these mistakes by not marking—by not "taking off"—for them? Putting dialect-based errors in perspective begins with recognizing that mere correctness does not make writing good. Unfortunately, the attitudes of most fully schooled American adults (and even some schoolteachers) testify to the contrary; it is one of the most embarrassing outcomes of our educational process that most graduates end up believing that writing well means writing without too many spelling, grammar, and punctuation errors. By this logic, all sorts of contemptible but carefully copy-edited prose fall into the category of "good writing," while brilliant or profound writing that contains many nonstandard-dialect features is by definition "bad."

But our standards of "good" and "bad" writing in school are peculiar in another way. A piece of student writing is judged "bad" when perhaps every tenth word contains an error or deviates somehow from standard written language. But notice what a lofty standard of correctness is being upheld here. In any other school subject—reading, mathematics, science, social studies—90 percent accuracy is considered *excellent*. Yet a student who produces the correct, conventional, or standard forms on 90 percent of words in a piece of school writing may well get an "F." The fact is that *we hold to a higher standard of perfection in the mechanics of writing than in any other school subject*. And this anomaly punishes—drastically and disproportionately—students whose home dialect happens to differ even slightly from the dialect approved by the school.

Teachers who are committed to a model of the writing process as a set of recursive stages, and who want students to develop the habit of revising their work carefully through multiple drafts, will avoid premature grading of works in progress. Once such an official and quantitative label has been affixed, something inside an author may withdraw from the work—and the future of the piece is jeopardized. Of course, students often become accomplices in their own oppression; after years in school they become grade-dependent and refuse to work at any task unless "paid" in the coin of letter grades. Skillful teachers realize that they must work with this very real dependency, either by devising experiences that wean students from their habit or else by simply "paying" for any substantially new draft with another grade. Both approaches can work.

Rather than an invariable obligation to judge, grading needs to be used as a selective, occasional, and well-timed opportunity to guide student writing. Some kinds of grading are clearly altogether inappropriate; there is little justification for awarding letter grades to students' personal reminiscences or fictional narratives. Not only is it unwise to risk this precious sharing of self with the potential wound of a grade, but there is little defensible basis for weighing one student's trip to the zoo against another's sick relative, unless the grade is assigned mostly on the basis of form, which is a counterproductive strategy in any case. Other modes of writing, particularly the transactional varieties, are much better suited to grading, and rational criteria can be developed for them. But the criteria will need to be different depending upon the task, subject, purpose, audience, and other aspects of the piece at hand. Just as in the real world, where the standards for a "good" writing performance vary according to the situation, so too should writing in school be evaluated not just on the quality of its content and form, but also by how appropriately the discourse is suited to the context for which it was created.

Cumulative grading of student writing is not particularly difficult to implement (Graves 1983, Daniels and Zemelman 1985). One useful practice is for the teacher and individual students to select from the student's writing folder the five or six pieces that represent his or her best (most fully polished, most satisfying to the author, etc.) pieces written over a marking period. These pieces are reviewed at a summary conference between the student and teacher at which they focus on the patterns and direction of growth. Then the teacher assigns a grade in accord with whatever standards prevail in his or her class. There are many other approaches to flexible and cumulative grading, and the best ones have one thing in common: they proceed from the assumption that the function of evaluation in writing is to help the next piece be better than the last one, that is, to be genuinely formative, and not just a judgment.

15. *Practicing and using writing as a tool of learning in all subjects across the curriculum, not just in English.*

The challenge of integrating writing activities into all school subjects returns us to the issue of teacher attitudes with which we began our list of factors. Developing writing across the curriculum, unlike most of the other ideas in this chapter, is an issue of administrative and faculty commitment in whole schools, not just a matter of the goodwill and good practice of individual teachers. If students are to fully appreciate the value of writing, and fully develop the range and depth of their own writing ability, they will need to gain experience in the widest possible array of real, meaningful, content-centered writing experience.

The pioneering studies of James Britton and his associates (1975) have documented the connection between writing activities and subject-matter learning. The problem lies in implementing a program. When subject-area teachers are exhorted to join up with a "writing-across-the-curriculum" effort, they are sometimes understandably suspicious that English teachers are trying to unload part of their own burden onto other departments and teachers. Yet some of the best possible writing experience can be provided by the real problems, puzzles, and challenges of the content of the other school subjects students need to study. Given an effective program of inservice training, subject-area teachers can be shown that certain writing activities really do help students to engage with and master the content of a subject. Realizing this, these teachers will "join up," embedding more writing into the learning activities of their courses.

As we come to understand and appreciate the complexity of writing as a language skill and as a school subject, we can only develop greater respect for the magnitude of the task of developing young writers. In a way, it is not surprising that our past efforts to teach writing have been so unsuccessful, realizing as we do now how inappropriate they were to the real nature of learning to write. Similarly, we now understand that to do a superior job of developing young writers, we will have to enlist more than just the English and language arts teachers. We need the assistance of all subject-area teachers, whose courses offer students wonderful opportunities to experiment with the real language, audiences, rules of evidence, and other elements of the field. Perhaps in order to draw these other teachers into the effort, we will need to share with them Fulwiler's (1979) and Wotring and Tierney's (1981) accounts of using learning logs to learn content, and the work of Weiss and Walters (1980) and Giroux (1979) on using writing to learn in social studies. Glatthorn (1981) has even shown that writing across the curriculum not only helps students learn content but also fosters better intraschool cooperation. Book-length treatments on the theory and practice of writing across the curriculum by Gere (1985), Fulwiler and Young (1982), and Mayher, Lester, and Pradl (1983) may help teachers in other disciplines to see the value of writing as an enrichment of their own teaching.

But beyond the involvement of other faculty, there is also a need for a broader and more institutional commitment to writing as a tool for learning, a kind of endorsement that needs to come from school principals and administrators. There needs to be both institutional support and assistance available for subject-area teachers who are integrating writing activities into their courses. Indeed, an official schoolwide focus on writing would not be too much to ask, especially in schools where literacy instruction poses a special and important challenge.

For the special groups of students we have been considering in this book, schools could probably offer no greater academic opportunity than an integrated and consistent program of writing experience throughout their secondary education. There is nothing more basic to success in high school itself, more closely tied to critical thinking, or more relevant to the prospect for higher education, than the ability to write. Another way of understanding the importance of this issue is to recognize that until we do begin teaching these students to write, they will not have received the equal educational opportunity which America claims to offer all of its children.

Bibliography

An asterisk next to an entry indicates that the resource is *practitioner-oriented.* Documents indexed in *Resources in Education (RIE)* are denoted by a 6-digit ED (ERIC Document) number. The majority of ERIC documents are reproduced on microfiche and may be viewed at ERIC collections in libraries and other institutions or can be ordered from the ERIC Document Reproduction Service (EDRS) in either paper copy or microfiche. For ordering information and price schedules write or call EDRS, 3900 Wheeler Avenue, Alexandria, VA 22304, 1-800-227-3742.

Articles annotated in *Current Index to Journals in Education (CIJE)* are denoted by a 6-digit EJ (ERIC Journal) number and may be obtained from a library collection, from the publisher, or from University Microfilms International, UMI Article Clearinghouse, 300 North Zeeb Road, Ann Arbor, MI 48106, 1-800-732-0616.

Adams, V. A. (1971). A study of the effects of two methods of teaching composition to twelfth graders. Diss., University of Illinois at Champaign-Urbana.

Anderson, V., C. Bereiter, and D. Smart (1980). Activation of semantic networks in writing: Teaching students how to do it themselves. Paper, Annual Meeting of the American Educational Research Association.

* Applebee, A. N. (1981). *Writing in the secondary school: English and the content areas.* Research report no. 21. Urbana, Ill.: National Council of Teachers of English.

—— (1984). *Contexts for learning to write: Studies of secondary school instruction. Writing research* series. Norwood, N.J.: Ablex Publishing Corp.

Applebee, A. N., J. A. Langer, and I. V. S. Mullis (1986). *Writing: Trends across the decade, 1974–84* (National Assessment of Educational Progress report). Princeton, N.J.: Educational Testing Service.

Arnold, L. V. (1963). Effects of frequency of writing and intensity of teacher evaluation upon performance in written composition of tenth grade students. *Dissertation Abstracts* 24: 1021-A.

Ash, S., and J. Myhill (1983). *Linguistic correlates of inter-ethnic contact* (Research report). Philadelphia: Linguistics Laboratory, University of Pennsylvania.

Bamberg, B. J. (1978). Composition instruction does make a difference: A comparison of the high school preparation of college freshmen in regular and remedial English classes. *Research in the Teaching of English* 12, no. 1: 47–59. EJ 179 132. ED 140 342.

Baron, D. E. (1982). *Grammar and good taste: Reforming the American language.* New Haven: Yale University Press.

Bartholomae, D. (1984). The study of error. *College Composition and Communication* 31: 253–69. EJ 236 378.

Baugh, J. (1983). *Black street speech: Its history, structure and survival.* Austin: University of Texas Press.

Beach, R. (1979). The effects of between-draft teacher evaluation versus student self-evaluation on high school students' revising of rough drafts. *Research in the Teaching of English* 13, no. 2: 111–19. EJ 204 586.

* Beaven, M. H. (1977). Individualized goal setting, self-evaluation, and peer evaluation. In *Evaluating writing: Describing, measuring, judging*, edited by C. R. Cooper and L. Odell, 135–56. Urbana, Ill.: National Council of Teachers of English.

Bereiter, C., M. Scardamalia, V. Anderson, and D. Smart (1980). An experiment in teaching abstract planning in writing. Paper, Annual Meeting of the American Educational Research Association.

Birnbaum, J. C. (1981). A study of reading and writing behaviors of selected fourth grade and seventh grade students. *Dissertation Abstracts International* 42: 152-A.

Blount, N. S. (1973). Research on teaching literature, language and composition. In *Second handbook of research on teaching*, edited by R. M. W. Travers, 1072–97. Chicago: Rand McNally & Co.

* Boyer, E. L. (1983). *High school: A report on secondary education in America.* New York: Harper & Row.

Braddock, R., R. Lloyd-Jones, and L. Schoer (1963). *Research in written composition.* Urbana, Ill.: National Council of Teachers of English. ED 003 374.

* Britton, J. N. (1970). *Language and learning.* Baltimore: Penguin Books.

* Britton, J. N., T. Burgess, N. Martin, A. McLeod, and H. Rosen. (1975). *The development of writing abilities: 11–18.* London: Macmillan Education Ltd. ED 144 049.

Bruffee, K. A. (1980). *A short course in writing.* Boston: Little, Brown & Co.

Bruner, J. S. (1962). *On knowing: Essays for the left hand.* Cambridge: Harvard University Press.

——— (1978). The role of dialogue in language acquisition. In *The child's conception of language*, edited by A. Sinclair, R. J. Jarvells, W. J. M. Levett. Berlin: Springer-Verlag.

* Burling, R. (1970). *English in black and white.* New York: Holt, Rinehart, & Winston. ED 095 529.

Burns, H. L., Jr. (1980). Stimulating rhetorical invention in English composition through computer-assisted instruction. ED 188 245.

* California State Department of Education (1982). *Handbook for planning an effective writing program.* Sacramento, Calif.: California State Department of Education.

Calkins, L. M. (1979). Andrea learns to make writing hard. *Language Arts* 56: 569–76.

——— (1980). When children want to punctuate: Basic skills belong in context. *Language Arts* 57: 567–73. ED 170 766.

* ——— (1983). *Lessons from a child: On the teaching and learning of writing.* Exeter, N.H.: Heinemann Educational Books.

Cazden, C. B., S. Michaels, and P. Tabors (1985). Spontaneous repairs in sharing time narratives: The intersection of metalinguistic awareness, speech event, and narrative style. In *The acquisition of written language: Response and revision,* edited by S. W. Freedman, 51–64. Norwood, N.J.: Ablex Publishing Corp. ED 265 553.

Chafe, W. L. (1982). Integration and involvement in speaking, writing, and oral literature. In *Spoken and written language: Exploring orality and literacy,* edited by D. Tannen, 35–54. Vol. IX of *Advances in discourse processes.* Norwood, N.J.: Ablex Publishing Corp.

* Chambers, J., and J. Bond, eds. (1983). *Black English: Educational equity and the law.* Ann Arbor, Mich.: Karoma Press.

Chomsky, N. (1965). *Aspects of the theory of syntax.* Cambridge: M.I.T. Press.

* Christensen, F. (1967). Notes toward a new rhetoric: Six essays for teachers. New York: Harper & Row. ED 029 891.

* Clifford, J. P. (1978). An experimental inquiry into the effectiveness of collaborative learning as a method for improving the experiential writing performance of college freshmen in a remedial writing class. *Dissertation Abstracts International* 38: 7289-A.

———— (1981). Composing in stages: The effects of a collaborative pedagogy. *Research in the Teaching of English* 15, no. 1: 37–53. EJ 242 211.

Coleman, D. R. (1982). The effects of pupil use of a creative writing scale as an evaluative and instructional tool by primary gifted students. *Dissertation Abstracts International* 42: 3409-A.

Combs, W. (1976). Further effects of sentence-combining practice on writing ability. *Research in the Teaching of English* 10, no. 2: 137–49. EJ 144 485.

* Cooper, C. R. (1973). Research roundup: Oral and written composition. *English Journal* 62: 1201–3. EJ 137 929.

———— (1974). Research roundup: Oral and written composition. *English Journal* 63, no. 6: 102–4.

* ———— (1975). Research roundup: Measuring growth in writing. *English Journal* 64, no. 3: 111–20. EJ 117 490.

Daniels, H. A. (1973). Bi-dialectalism: A policy analysis. Ann Arbor, Mich.: University Microfilms. ED 089 219.

———— (1983). *Famous last words: The American language crisis reconsidered.* Carbondale, Ill.: Southern Illinois University Press.

Daniels, H. A. and S. Zemelman (1985). *A writing project: Training teachers of composition from kindergarten to college.* Exeter, N.H.: Heinemann Educational Books. ED 257 110.

Diederich, P. B. (1974). *Measuring growth in English.* Urbana, Ill.: National Council of Teachers of English. ED 097 702.

Dieterich, D. J. (1972). Composition evaluation: Options and advice. *English Journal* 61: 1264–71. EJ 070 502.

Dow, R. H. (1973). The student-writer's laboratory: An approach to composition. *Dissertation Abstracts International* 34: 2435-A.

Drake, G. (1974). The source of American linguistic prescriptivism. Paper, Annual Meeting of Linguistic Society of America.

Ebel, R. L., ed. (1969). *Encyclopedia of Educational research.* New York: Macmillan Publishing. ED 040 587.

* Elbow, P. (1973). *Writing without teachers.* New York: Oxford University Press. ED 078 431.

Elley, W. B., I. H. Barham, H. Lamb, and M. Wylie (1976). The role of grammar in a secondary school English curriculum. *Research in the Teaching of English* 10, no. 1: 5–21. EJ 112 410. ED 144 474.

* Emig, J. (1971). *The composing processes of twelfth graders.* Research report no. 13. Urbana, Ill.: National Council of Teachers of English. ED 058 205.

——— (1982). Writing, composition, and rhetoric. In *Encyclopedia of educational research,* edited by H. T. Mitzel, 2021–31. New York: Macmillan Publishing.

Erickson, F. (1984). Rhetoric, anecdote, and rhapsody: Coherence strategies in a conversation among black American adolescents. In *Coherence in spoken and written discourse,* edited by D. Tannen, 81–154. Vol. XII of *Advances in discourse processes.* Norwood, N.J.: Ablex Publishing Corp.

* Eschholz, P. A. (1980). The prose models approach: Using products in the process. In *Eight approaches to teaching composition,* edited by T. R. Donovan and B. W. McClelland, 21–36. Urbana, Ill.: National Council of Teachers of English.

Faigley, L., and S. Witte (1981). Analyzing revision. *College Composition and Communication* 32: 400–14. EJ 256 237.

* Falk, J. S. (1979). Language acquisition and the teaching and learning of writing. *College English* 41: 436–37. EJ 217 521.

Farr, M. (1985a). *Advances in writing research: Children's early writing development.* Writing research series. Norwood, N.J.: Ablex Publishing Corp.

———(1985b). Review of J. Chambers (ed.), *Black English: Educational equity and the law. Language in Society* 14: 108–13.

Farr, M., and M. A. Janda (1985). Basic writing students: Investigating oral and written language. *Research in the Teaching of English* 19, no. 1: 62–83. EJ 309 865.

Farr Whiteman, M. (1981a). Dialect influence in writing. In *Variation in writing: Functional and linguistic-cultural differences,* edited by M. Farr Whiteman, 153–66. Hillsdale, N.J.: Lawrence Erlbaum Associates. ED 214 204.

* ——— ed. (1980). *Reactions to Ann Arbor: Vernacular Black English and education.* Washington, D.C.: Center for Applied Linguistics. ED 197 624.

———, ed. (1981b). *Variation in writing: Functional and linguistic-cultural differences.* Vol. 1 of *Writing: The nature, development, and teaching of written communication.* Hillsdale, N.J.: Lawrence Erlbaum Associates. ED 214 204.

Ferguson, C. (1977). Linguistic theory. In *Bilingual education, Current perspectives: Linguistics,* 43–52. Washington, D.C.: Center for Applied Linguistics.

* Florio, S. (1979). The problem of dead letters: Social perspectives on the teaching of writing. *Elementary School Journal* 80, no. 1: 1–7. EJ 222 287.

Florio, S. and C. M. Clark (1982a). The functions of writing in an elementary classroom. *Research in the Teaching of English* 16, no. 2: 115–30. EJ 261 477.

—— (1982b). What is writing for? Writing in the first weeks of school in a second-third grade classroom. In *Communicating in the classroom*, edited by L. C. Wilkinson, 265-82. *Language, thought, and culture* series. New York: Academic Press.

Flower, L. S., and J. R. Hayes (1981a). A cognitive process theory of writing. *College Composition and Communication* 32, no. 4: 365-87.

—— (1981b). Plans that guide the composing process. In *Writing: The nature, development, and teaching of written communication*, Vol. 2, edited by C. H. Frederiksen and J. F. Dominic, 39-58. Hillsdale, N.J.: Lawrence Erlbaum Associates. ED 221 888.

Freedman, S. W., C. Greenleaf, M. Sperling, and L. Parker (1985). *The role of response in the acquisition of written language*. Final report. NIE Grant No. G-083-0065. ED 260 407.

* Fulwiler, T. E. (1979). Journal-writing across the curriculum. In *Classroom practices in the teaching of English, 1979-80: How to handle the paper load*, 15-22. Urbana, Ill.: National Council of Teachers of English.

—— (1981). Showing, not telling, at a writing workshop. *College English* 43, no. 1: 55-63. EJ 240 380.

* Fulwiler, T. E., and A. Young, eds. (1982). *Language connections: Writing and reading across the curriculum*. Urbana, Ill.: National Council of Teachers of English.

* Gere, A. R., ed. (1985). *Roots in the sawdust: Writing to learn across the disciplines*. Urbana, Ill.: National Council of Teachers of English.

Gilmore, P., and D. M. Smith (1982). A retrospective discussion of the state of the art in ethnography and education. In *Children in and out of school: Ethnography and education*, edited by P. Gilmore and A. A. Glatthorn, 3-18. Washington, D.C.: Center for Applied Linguistics.

* Giroux, H. A. (1979). Teaching content and thinking through writing. *Social Education* 43, no. 3: 190-93. EJ 198 672.

* Glatthorn, A. A. (1981). *Writing in the schools: Improvement through effective leadership*. Reston, Va.: National Association of Secondary School Principals. ED 208 416.

* Goodlad, J. I. (1984). *A place called school: Prospects for the future*. New York: McGraw-Hill. ED 236 137.

Goodman, Y., and others (1984). *A two-year case study observing the development of third and fourth grade Native American children's writing processes*. NIE Grant No. G-81-0127. Washington, D.C.: National Institute of Education. ED 241 240.

Goody, J., and I. Watt (1963). The consequences of literacy. *Comparative Studies in Society and History* 5, no. 3: 304-45.

Graff, D., W. Labov, and W. Harris (1983). Testing listeners' reactions to phonological markers of ethnic identity: A new method for sociolinguistic research. Paper, Annual Conference on New Ways of Analyzing Variation in English, Montreal.

* Graves, D. H. (1978). *Balance the basics: Let them write*. New York: Ford Foundation. ED 192 364.

* —— (1983). *Writing: Teachers and children at work*. Exeter, N.H.: Heinemann Educational Books. ED 234 430.

————, ed. (1982). *A case study observing the development of primary children's composing, spelling, and motor behaviors during the writing process.* Final report. NIE Grant No. G-78-0174. Durham, N.H.: University of New Hampshire. ED 218 653.

Greenberg, J. H., ed. (1963). *Universals of language.* Cambridge, Mass.: M.I.T. Press.

* Haas, V. J., P. R. Childers, E. Babbit, and S. M. Dylla (1972). English composition by workshop. *Journal of Experimental Education* 40, no. 3: 33–37. EJ 055 178.

* Hailey, J. (1978). *Teaching writing K–8.* Berkeley: University of California. ED 246 439.

Halliday, M. A. K., and R. Hasan (1976). *Cohesion in English.* New York: Longman.

* Hansen, B. (1978). Rewriting is a waste of time. *College English* 39: 956–60. EJ 181 287.

* Harste, J. C., V. Woodward, and C. Burke (1984). *Language stories and literacy lessons.* Exeter, N.H.: Heinemann Educational Books. ED 257 113.

Hartwell, P. (1980). Dialect interference in writing: A critical view. *Research in the Teaching of English* 14, no. 2: 101–18. EJ 225 425.

* ———— (1985). Grammar, grammars, and the teaching of grammar. *College English* 47, no. 2: 105–27. EJ 311 538.

Hatfield, W. (1935). *An experience curriculum in English.* New York: Appleton-Century Company.

Haugen, E. (1959). Planning for a standard language in modern Norway. *Anthropological Linguistics* 1, no. 3: 8–21.

———— (1966). Linguistics and language planning. In *Sociolinguistics,* edited by W. Bright, 50–71. The Hague: Mouton.

Hayes, J. R., and Flower, L. S. (1981). Identifying the organization of writing processes. In *Cognitive processes in writing: An interdisciplinary approach,* edited by L. W. Gregg and E. R. Steinberg, 3–30. Hillsdale, N.J.: Lawrence Erlbaum Associates.

* Haynes, E. F. (1978). Using research in preparing to teach writing. *English Journal* 67, no. 1: 82–88. EJ 175 449.

Hays, J. N. (1981). The effect of audience considerations upon the revisions of a group of basic writers and more competent junior and senior writers. Paper, Annual Meeting of the Conference on College Composition and Communication. ED 204 802.

Heath, S. B. (1980). Standard English: Biography of a symbol. In *Standards and Dialects in English,* edited by T. Chopen and J. M. Williams, 53–82. Cambridge, Mass.: Winthrop.

———— (1981). Oral and literate traditions—Endless linkages. In *Moving between practice and research in writing,* edited by A. Humes and others, 21–34. Los Alamitos, Calif.: Southwest Regional Laboratory for Educational Research and Development. ED 198 569.

* ———— (1983). *Ways with words: Language, life, and work in communities and classrooms.* Cambridge: Cambridge University Press.

Heath, S. B., and A. Branscombe (1985). "Intelligent writing" in an audience community: Teacher, students, and researcher. In *The acquisition of written language: Response and revision*, edited by S. W. Freedman, 3–32. *Writing research* series. Norwood, N.J.: Ablex Publishing Corp.

Heys, F., Jr. (1962). The theme-a-week assumption: A report of an experiment. *English Journal* 51: 320–22.

Hillocks, G., Jr. (1982). The interaction of instruction, teacher comment, and revision in teaching the composing process. *Research in the Teaching of English* 16, no. 3: 261–78. EJ 268 134.

* ——— (1986). *Research on written composition: New directions for teaching.* Urbana, Ill.: National Conference on Research in English and ERIC Clearinghouse on Reading and Communication Skills. ED 265 552.

Hirsch, E. D., Jr., (1977). *The philosophy of composition.* Chicago: University of Chicago Press. ED 145 468.

Hunt, K. W. (1970). *Syntactic maturity in schoolchildren and adults.* Monograph of the Society for Research in Child Development, Vol. 35, serial 134, no. 1. Chicago: University of Chicago Press.

* Judy, S. N. (1980). *The ABC's of literacy: A guide for parents and educators.* New York: Oxford University Press. ED 178 950.

King, M. and V. M. Rentel (1981). *How children learn to write: A longitudinal study.* Final report. NIE Grant Nos. G-79-0137 and G-79-0039. Columbus: Ohio State University. ED 213 050.

——— (1982). *Transition to writing.* Final report. NIE Grant Nos. G-79-0137 and G-79-0031. Columbus: Ohio State University. ED 240 603.

——— (1983). *A longitudinal study of coherence in children's written narratives.* Final report. NIE Grant No. G-81-0063. Columbus: Ohio State University. ED 237 989.

Kinneavy, J. L. (1971). *A theory of discourse: The aims of discourse.* Englewood Cliffs, N.J.: Prentice-Hall. ED 076 992.

* Kochman, T. (1972a). Toward an ethnography of black American speech behavior. In *Rappin' and stylin' out: Communication in urban black America*, edited by T. Kochman, 241–64. Urbana, Ill.: University of Illinois Press.

——— (1981). *Black and white styles in conflict.* Chicago: University of Chicago Press.

* ———, ed. (1972b). *Rappin' and stylin' out: Communication in urban black America.* Urbana, Ill.: University of Illinois Press.

Labov, W. (1964). Phonological correlates of social stratification. *American Anthropologist* 66, no. 6, Part 2: 164–76.

——— (1969). Contraction, deletion, and inherent variability of the English copula. *Language* 45: 715–62.

* ——— (1970). *The study of nonstandard English.* Urbana, Ill.: National Council of Teachers of English. ED 024 053.

* ——— (1972a). *Language in the inner city: Studies in the Black English Vernacular.* Philadelphia: University of Pennsylvania Press. ED 082 196.

—— (1972b). *Sociolinguistic patterns.* Philadelphia: University of Pennsylvania Press.

——, ed. (1983). Recognizing Black English in the classroom. In *Black English: Educational equity and the law,* edited by J. Chambers and J. Bond, 29–55. Ann Arbor, Mich.: Karoma Press.

Labov, W., and W. Harris (1983). De facto segregation of black and white vernaculars. Paper, Annual Conference on New Ways of Analyzing Variation in English, Montreal.

Lagana, J. R. (1972). The development, implementation, and evaluation of a model for teaching composition which utilizes individualized learning and peer grouping. *Dissertation Abstracts International* 33: 4063-A. ED 079 726.

Levinson, S. C. (1983). *Pragmatics.* Cambridge: Cambridge University Press.

* Mayher, J. S., N. Lester, and G. Pradl (1983). *Learning to write/Writing to learn.* Upper Montclair, N.J.: Boynton/Cook. ED 236 695.

Mellon, J. C. (1969). *Transformational sentence-combining: A method for enhancing the development of syntactic fluency in English composition.* Urbana, Ill.: National Council of Teachers of English. ED 018 405.

Michaels, S. (1981). "Sharing time": Children's narrative styles and differential access to literacy. *Language in Society* 10: 423–42.

Michaels, S., and J. Collins (1984). Oral discourse styles: Classroom interaction and the acquisition of literacy. In *Coherence in spoken and written discourse,* edited by D. Tannen, 219–44. Vol. 12 of *Advances in discourse processes.* Norwood, N.J.: Ablex Publishing Corp.

Moffett, J. W. (1968). *Teaching the universe of discourse.* Boston: Houghton Mifflin.

* Moffett, J. W., and B. J. Wagner (1976). *Student-centered language arts and reading, K-13: A handbook for teachers.* Boston: Houghton Mifflin. ED 030 665.

Morenberg, M. (1980). Sentence combining over a three-year period: A case study. Paper, Annual Meeting of the Conference on College Composition and Communication. ED 186 921.

* Murray, D. M. (1968). *A writer teaches writing.* Boston: Houghton Mifflin.

Myhill, J., and W. Harris (1983). The use of the verbal -s inflection in BEV. Paper, Annual Conference on New Ways of Analyzing Variation in English, Montreal.

* National Assessment of Educational Progress (1981). *Highlights and trends: Writing achievement, 1969-79.* Denver, Colo.: Education Commission of the States.

O'Hare, F. (1973). *Sentence combining: Improving student writing without formal grammar instruction.* Research report no. 15. Urbana, Ill.: National Council of Teachers of English.

Odell, L. (1974). Measuring the effect of instruction in pre-writing. *Research in the Teaching of English* 8, no. 2: 228–40. EJ 105 719.

Ogbu, J. U. (1974). *The next generation: An ethnography of education in an urban neighborhood.* New York: Academic Press. ED 091 481.

—— (1980). Literacy in subordinate cultures: The case of black Americans. Manuscript prepared for Literacy Conference, Library of Congress, Washington, D.C.

Olson, D. R. (1977). From utterance to text: The bias of language in speech and writing. *Harvard Educational Review* 47, no. 3: 257–81. EJ 167 140.

* Perl, S. (1980). Understanding composing. *College Composition and Communication* 31: 363–69. EJ 240 354.

—— (1985). *Portraits of writing teachers at work.* Final report to the National Institute of Education. New York: Herbert H. Lehman College, City University of New York.

Perl, S., and others (1983). How teachers teach the writing process: Overview of an ethnographic research project. *Elementary School Journal* 84, no. 1: 19–44.

* Perl, S., and N. Wilson (1986). *Through teachers' eyes.* Exeter, N.H.: Heinemann Educational Books.

* Petrosky, A. (1977). Grammar instruction: What we know (Research roundup). *English Journal* 66, no. 9: 86–88. EJ 173 297.

Philips, S. U. (1972). Participant structures and communicative competence: Warm Springs children in community and classroom. In *Functions of language in the classroom,* edited by C. Cazden, V.P. John, and D. Hymes, 370–94. New York: Teachers College Press. See also EJ 309 263.

—— (1983). *The invisible culture: Communication in classroom and community on the Warm Springs Indian Reservation.* New York: Longman.

Rohman, D. G., and A. O. Wlecke (1964). *Pre-writing: The construction and application of models for concept formation in writing.* U.S. Office of Education Cooperative Research Project No. 2174. East Lansing, Mich.: Michigan State University. ED 001 273.

* Rosenthal, R., and L. F. Jacobson (1968). Teacher expectations for the disadvantaged. *Scientific American* 218, no. 4: 19–23.

Sager, C. (1973). Improving the quality of written composition through pupil use of rating scale. Paper, Annual Meeting of the National Council of Teachers of English. ED 089 304.

Sawkins, M. W. (1971). The oral responses of selected fifth grade children to questions concerning their written expression. *Dissertation Abstracts International* 31: 6287-A. ED 057 046.

Scardamalia, M., C. Bereiter, and H. Goelman (1982). The role of production factors in writing ability. In *What writers know: The language, process and structure of written discourse,* edited by M. Nystrand, 173–210. New York: Academic Press.

Scollon, R., and S. B. Scollon (1981). *Narrative, literacy and face in interethnic communication.* Vol. VII of *Advances in discourse processes.* Norwood, N.J.: Ablex Publishing Corp.

* Shaughnessy, M. P. (1977). *Errors and expectations: A guide for the teacher of basic writing.* New York: Oxford University Press.

Sizer, T. R. (1984). *Horace's compromise: The dilemma of the American high school.* Boston: Houghton Mifflin.

Sledd, J. (1972). Doublespeak: Dialectology in the service of big brother. *College English* 33: 439–56. EJ 049 134.

* Smitherman, G. (1977). *Talkin' and testifyin': The language of black America.* Boston: Houghton Mifflin.

Sommers, N. I. (1979). Revision in the composing process: A case study of college freshmen and experienced adult writers. *Dissertation Abstracts International* 39: 5374-A.

* Sowers, S. (1979). A six-year-old's writing process: The first half of first grade. *Language Arts* 56: 829-35.

Stallard, C. K. (1974). An analysis of the writing behavior of good student writers. *Research in the Teaching of English* 8, no. 2: 206-18.

Staton, J. (1982). *Analysis of dialogue journal writing as a communicative event.* Final report. NIE Grant No. G-80-0122. Washington, D.C.: Center for Applied Linguistics. ED 214 196 and ED 214 197.

Staton, J., R. W. Shuy, J. K. Peyton, and L. Reed (in press). *Dialogue journal communication: Classroom, linguistic, social and cognitive views. Writing research* series. Norwood, N.J.: Ablex Publishing Corp.

Stotsky, S. L. (1975). Sentence combining as a curricular activity: Its effect on written language development and reading comprehension. *Research in the Teaching of English* 9: 30-71. EJ 130 870.

Street, B. V. (1984). *Literacy in theory and practice.* Cambridge: Cambridge University Press.

Strom, D. (1960). Research in grammar and usage and its implications for teaching writing. *Bulletin of the School of Education, Indiana University* 36, no. 5: entire issue.

Tannen, D. (1982a). Oral and literate strategies in spoken and written narratives. *Language* 58, no. 1: 1-21. EJ 259 858.

———— (1982b). The oral/literate continuum in discourse. In *Spoken and written language: Exploring orality and literacy,* edited by D. Tannen, 1-16. Norwood, N.J.: Ablex Publishing Corp.

————, ed. (1982c). *Spoken and written language: Exploring orality and literacy.* Vol. IX of *Advances in discourse processes.* Norwood, N.J.: Ablex Publishing Corp.

* Taylor, O. L. (1983). Black English: An agenda for the 1980's. In *Black English: Educational equity and the law,* edited by J. Chambers and J. Bond, 133-43. Ann Arbor, Mich.: Karoma Press.

* Tchudi, S. N., and S. J. Tchudi (1983). *Teaching writing in the content areas: Elementary school, middle school/junior high, senior high school.* (3 vols.). Washington, D.C.: National Education Association. ED 232 211, ED 232 213, and ED 232 212.

Teale, W., and E. Sulzby, eds. (1986). *Emergent literacy: Writing and reading. Writing research* series. Norwood, N.J.: Ablex Publishing Corp.

Traugott, E. (1981). The voice of varied linguistic and cultural groups in fiction: Some criteria for the use of language varieties in writing. In *Variation in writing: Functional and linguistic-cultural differences,* edited by M. Farr Whiteman, 111-36. Hillsdale, N.J.: Lawrence Erlbaum Associates.

* VanDeWeghe, R. (1978). "Research in written composition": Fifteen years of investigation. ED 157 095.

Weiss, R. H., and S. A. Walters (1980). Writing apprehension: Implications for teaching, writing, and concept clarity. Paper, Annual Meeting of the Conference on College Composition and Communication. ED 189 619.

* Williams, F. (1976). *Explorations of the linguistic attitudes of teachers.* Rowley, Mass.: Newbury House. ED 146 797.

Wolfram, W. A., and R. W. Fasold (1974). *The study of social dialects in American English.* Englewood Cliffs, N.J.: Prentice-Hall.

* Wolfram, W., and M. Whiteman (1971). The role of dialect interference in composition. *The Florida FL Reporter* 9, no. 1-2: 34-38, 59. EJ 052 149.

* Wotring, A. M., and R. Tierney (1981). *Two studies of writing in high school science.* Classroom research study No. 5. Berkeley, Calif.: Bay Area Writing Project. ED 238 725.

Young, R. E., and F. M. Koen (1973). *The tagmemic discovery procedure: An evaluation of its uses in the teaching of rhetoric.* ED 084 517.

Authors

Marcia Farr is an associate professor of English at the University of Illinois at Chicago, where she teaches and conducts research on theoretical and pedagogical issues in literacy use and acquisition. She was previously at the National Institute of Education, where she developed a national research program on writing and served as the government spokesperson on the "Ann Arbor Case" involving the teaching of standard written English to speakers of Vernacular Black English. Farr has taught at the secondary level and has designed and taught inservice workshops on nonstandard dialects and language arts instruction. She is series editor of *Writing Research: Multidisciplinary Inquiries into the Nature of Writing* (Ablex Publishing Corp.) and has given numerous public presentations on writing and sociolinguistic issues to a wide variety of audiences.

Harvey Daniels is an associate professor on the graduate faculty of the National College of Education and is co-director of the Illinois Writing Project. He has conducted extensive inservice programs in composition and in writing across the curriculum. Daniels has taught English to inner-city students at the secondary level and has contributed numerous articles on language, literacy, and teaching issues to both the popular press and professional journals. He is the author, with Steven Zemelman, of *A Writing Project: Training Teachers of Composition from Kindergarten through College* (Heinemann Educational Books, 1985), and of *Famous Last Words: The American Language Crisis Reconsidered* (Southern Illinois University Press, 1983).